Organisational Change: Ma]

ISBN: 979-8-69099

Copyright © John M. Wilson (2020).

First published 2020.

The right of John M. Wilson to be identified as the author of this work has been asserted by him in accordance with the Copyright, Designs and Patents Act 1988.

All rights reserved. No part of this publication may be produced, stored in a retrieval system, or transmitted in any other form or by any means, without the prior written permission of John M. Wilson.

Contents

Introduction	5
My Story	8
1. What it's like when change works for you	9
2. Why the current approach won't let you get there	11
It misses too many targets too often	11
It doesn't address the underlying cause	12
It traps you in a cycle of failure	12
It stops you exploiting synergies	14
Chapter summary	15
3: Mindset pre-requisites for changing approach	16
The principles of portfolio management	17
Air Traffic Control	17
The power of six	18
Top-down collective responsibility, not silos	19
'Change' is 'Business as Usual'	21
Spring clean all year round	22
Only people make things happen	23
Small is beautiful	24
Procrastination is the enemy of change	25

Chapter summary	26

4: How to turn the cycle of failure into a cycle of success — 27

Make the workload manageable	27
Determine and support organisational constraints – Supply	29
Define and manage organisational ambitions – Demand	38
Balance the two in a rolling portfolio plan of 'now, next, later'	51
Chapter summary	63

5: How to keep the cycle of success turning faster — 64

Use streamlined governance	64
Set up an Investment Authority (IA)	67
Build and activate an Investment Management Facility (IMF)	70
Embed the approach in 'the company way'	85
Continue to grow capability	86
Keep it fit and healthy	89
Chapter summary	94

Summary — 96

And finally — 98

Acknowledgements — 99

Index of Illustrations and tables — 100

Illustrations — 100

Tables 100

References 101

Introduction

Dear Reader,

As we enter the third decade of the 21st century, the delivery of organisational change is performing no better now than it was when we entered the first. Projects and programmes still fail at a rate of around 70%, yet organisations have spent the last twenty years and more trying to fix this. Whatever they've done clearly hasn't worked as intended. This failure to make a breakthrough has been a source of frustration for business leaders for as long as I can remember. And no wonder. Apart from the disappointment at not being able to readily take advantage of opportunities, fend off threats and grow at the rate that didn't seem beyond the realms of reasonableness, literally millions have been spent trying to improve delivery performance, but with seemingly little impact. Having been involved in the thick of it, I know what it feels like – pedalling furiously on a bicycle when the chain is off the cogs. Plenty of energy, little progression. Fortunately, my experience has also taught me what it takes to put the chain in place and keep it there. And how to make use of the gears to get much more for your efforts. I'm sharing it all in this book.

At the time of writing it is apparent that the need for organisations to be highly effective at delivering change has never been greater. And there's every indication it will get greater yet. The challenges were already coming thick and fast: Tough competition, cost pressures, digitalisation, cyber security, regulatory requirements, dynamic customer service expectations, industry consolidation (mergers and acquisitions) to name a few. Then along came COVID-19. The most effective weapon organisations have at their disposal to overcome these tough challenges, is change. So, they need to embrace it and make it work for them.

At its 2020 Annual Meeting, attended by more than 3000 people from 117 countries covering business, public services, politics and the arts, the World Economic Forum discussed the need for all companies, regardless of their starting positions, to continually reinvent themselves for sustained success in the competitive environment that lay ahead. And that was before the COVID pandemic took off. Recently the Harvard Business Review reported that it had found over half the clients they surveyed believed that they needed to reinvent their businesses every three years or less. The Boston Consulting

Group (BCG) said that to succeed in the coming years, organisations must learn to excel at ongoing change, even when all is going well. The message is clear: Organisations that resist change, unless blessed with some magical power, will expire; it's just a matter of time. Those that regard it as a distraction that they attend to reluctantly, may survive, if they are lucky. Those that become adept at using it and make it work for them have the best chance of long-lasting success.

This book will help you get change working for you, by making it consistently hit targets, generate even more value by exploiting the advantages that synergies offer and help you continue to get better at doing both. This will only happen if you embrace change as a holistic and joined-up investment in the future of your organisation. You will need to change your approach, and that in turn requires a shift in perspective.

The good news is that the book will show you how this can be accomplished in a matter of weeks by following a few simple steps and leveraging what you already have in place. You won't need a major transformation, a fancy new method, or an extensive training programme. What you will need is an entrepreneurial spirit, collaborative leadership, common sense, and pragmatic application of sound principles. By adopting a fresh perspective and a willingness to act, you will soon be exploiting what you have at your disposal and unleashing its potential to get more value realised sooner and more frequently.

If you haven't already, take a look now at the contents page at the beginning of the book. It's designed to take you through the journey at a headline level, from constant failure to constant success. What is covered can be applied to all organisations that run projects and programmes, regardless of industry or sector, whether they are commercial enterprises or not-for-profit, from the small concern to the major global player. You simply need to tailor the guidance to suit your circumstances. You will be encouraged to think, to challenge, to apply and to learn about how change can support your organisation in achieving its ambitions on an ongoing basis. You will become self-sufficient by doing so.

This book isn't the product of academic research or a critique of other's observations. It is the culmination of personal experience gained over nearly thirty years in the front line: Delivering and improving the capability to deliver change in extremely challenging conditions; in organisations reluctant to deviate from the comfort of an historic approach, despite its obvious failures. It is thus based on extensive learning and application on the job. There's no more authentic account of what it's like to make change work for you.

The impact of COVID-19 on everyday life and the business world has been one of the biggest in a generation. It has forced organisations into accepting challenging market conditions and different working arrangements, much of which will continue. In many cases, the impact has made the backlog of change and the challenges for the coming year even more overwhelming than usual, in part by slowing things down and putting more pressure on next year's plans and budgets, and in part by driving a whole new set of pressing requirements to operate effectively in a post COVID world. It is vital that organisations find a way to emerge from this, and in good shape. The faster and more effectively they can change, the better placed they will be. Smart organisations will grab this opportunity. The rest will bide their time while they wait to pick up from where they left off. Now is your chance to be smart…

My Story

I've spent nearly thirty years in organisational change and occupied most of the leadership roles from project manager through to change director. I've worked alongside many consultancies, from the boutique to the big 4. And I've worked in organisations as a consultant. My career has been largely in financial services, but I've also spent time in central government, defence and security, and early on in publishing. I've learned a lot from the diversity of the industries, sectors, the people and consultancies I've worked with and how they all grapple with basically the same problem – getting change done.

In that time, I've delivered a great many projects, programmes and portfolios successfully, and led significant improvements to delivery capability; setting up and running central change functions, Portfolio, Programme and Project Offices (PMOs and P3Os), and governance frameworks, and leading the provision of training and development. I've also led development of business strategy, which along with applying learning from an MBA, gave me a much broader and deeper understanding of the context that drives the need for change and the critical role it plays in making organisations successful.

I've often had to drive capability improvements as a pioneer, without much authority to corral support, so had to rely on influencing and persuasion and proving what will work rather than just articulating it. Mostly, it's been great fun and highly satisfying, at times though it's been very tough, and I've acquired plenty of battle scars and bullet wounds along the way. It's an experience that has helped me learn what does and doesn't work and how to produce the right results quickly. In the last 10 years or so I've learned not only how the effective application of portfolio management can truly enable long-lasting success, but why so few organisations readily take advantage of it.

So, what I share in this book is literally decades of first-hand experience in the field about how to make change work for you. It's about as authentic an account as you can get. I do hope you enjoy reading it and that you benefit greatly from it. It's offered with one aim only – to make you successful. Continuously.

Many thanks for reading,

John.

1. What it's like when change works for you

You work in an organisation that gets things done. Always. It readily adapts to take advantage of opportunities and fend off threats when it chooses to without disrupting day-to-day output. It never stops getting better at doing this because it never stops learning. Consequently, it always hits its targets and gets the expected return on its investments. And collectively the investments add up to more than the sum of the parts because it's adept at exploiting synergies. It regularly feels a sense of achievement, is trusted and respected by customers, investors, and the wider business community and it's a great place to work. This gives it confidence to be more adventurous and take on tougher challenges, with bigger prizes than the competition, which often it wins. As a result, it's a leader in its field.

In this organisation change is embedded in everything it does, psychologically, culturally and operationally – it's in the organisation's DNA. The 'change' plan is the 'business investment' plan, it is ongoing, not annual and it can readily adjust it to anticipate changes in circumstances. It is the rolling portfolio of investments that takes the organisation to where it wants to be at any given time. The realisation of value from this is constant. There are no crises, there are challenges, which it relishes because they are seen as opportunities to get further ahead. And there is nothing in the investment plan that doesn't add value.

There isn't a change department as such, everyone is a change agent and there is a network of technical 'change specialists' that can be grouped or dispersed, or a mixture of the two, as circumstances require. The checks and balances in place as part of governance are predicated on facilitating success rather than preventing failure, and they keep the organisation moving forward at an enviable pace. It uses a variety of methods, tools and practices to suit the circumstances, all with an emphasis on speed and accuracy to serve the organisation's ambitions. There's no room for emotional attachment to these – they serve a purpose, or they don't get used. At the heart of the organisation is an investment management capability that aligns its ambitions, its strategy, its end-to-end operations and the investment required in its future. This capability gives it an unshakeable advantage in the marketplace.

This might seem like the stuff of dreams. But all great achievements were dreams once. The trick is to turn them into reality.

As far as change is concerned, every organisation has the potential to do just that. Including yours. Want to know how? Read on…

2. Why the current approach won't let you get there

It misses too many targets too often

The failure rate of projects and programmes is still widely reported at around 70%. The Standish Group CHAOS report has been showing this regularly for the last twenty years or so. It's based on around 50,000 projects. The consulting group BCG recently put the failure rate at 75%. In 2018 Gartner found that 'clear success' could only be claimed in 34% of projects and in the APM's report on *Conditions for Project Success*, it claims nearly 80% of projects fail to wholly meet their planned objectives. First-hand experience in the last thirty years has shown these figures to be a reasonable assessment. This is clearly not good enough. Whatever the precise figure is, there is undoubtedly plenty of room for improvement.

Just think for a moment how much value is being lost. A 70% failure rate means that only 30% of projects will produce what you were expecting. The 30% are more likely to be smaller and simpler projects, along with perhaps some highly sensitive regulatory initiatives. The larger, more complex programmes, and consequently the most expensive, taking the lion's share of the organisation's investment, and expected to deliver the lion's share of the outcomes, are more likely to feature amongst the 70%. This is not only a pitifully poor return, but it leaves in place the cost of missed opportunities, unmitigated risks, prolonged inefficiencies and sub-optimal performance that the change was supposed to address.

Of course, there will be justification for shortfalls and variations from the original targets – things change. But ask yourself if you get what you need, when you need it. Too often the answer is no. And whilst this rate of failure remains, your organisation will be severely limited in what it can achieve – change is sapping your strength when it should be making you stronger – you are working for change not change for you.

This record of failure persists despite organisations having spent a fortune in effort, time and money year after year trying to improve delivery performance. If this had been effective in targeting the underlying cause, the failure rate would be in single figures by now.

It doesn't address the underlying cause

So, why hasn't it been effective? Unfortunately, most of the remedial action is spent tackling the symptoms rather than the cause. Too many targets are missed too often because the right amount of the right skills at the right time to get things right are not applied. And overloaded parts of the supply chain slow things down as initiatives have to wait for shared resource to become available.

This is caused by trying to do more than you have capacity for, which is driven by having so many top priority and urgent project and programmes. And the reason so many of them are top priority and urgent is because there is an ever-increasing backlog of overdue initiatives, which is caused by…too many targets having been missed. The key to unlock this is getting the workload to a manageable level. This is a portfolio management problem, not a project and programme delivery problem.

The impact of leaving this unaddressed is devastating and long-term. As the backlog continues to grow, so the proportion of 'new' investments continues to diminish. Eventually it will be next to nothing. The longer the problem remains unaddressed, the worse it will get. Furthermore, because so many projects and programmes are hanging around longer than expected, the priorities become driven by delivery pressures rather than the value of investment returns. You find that you are constantly playing catch up with yesterday when you should be getting ahead of tomorrow. You are losing advantage and are no longer in control of your future – you are working for the portfolio, not the portfolio working for you. Anyone who has a portfolio that looks very familiar year after year is almost certainly suffering from this problem.

It traps you in a cycle of failure

The irony is that whilst many organisations recognise that they are trying to do too much, the current approach prevents them from seeing it as the underlying cause of continued failure. This is because:

- Most organisations think of change as projects and programmes, much of which they run in silos – portfolios are regarded as simply lists of projects and programmes.

- The delivery problem manifests itself at the project and programme level, so that's where attention is drawn to.

- There is in any case room for improvement in project and programme delivery.

- So much on the 'to do' list is top priority and urgent – postponing anything is at odds with what most leaders are tasked with.

- The prevailing narrative is one of having to deal with 'constant change', so a heavy change workload is seen as a positive endorsement of the approach.

- Most of those involved have come to accept that doing too much is an uncomfortable necessity in the world of change today.

As such organisations continue to tackle the symptoms and so have trapped themselves in a cycle of failure.

THE CYCLE OF FAILURE

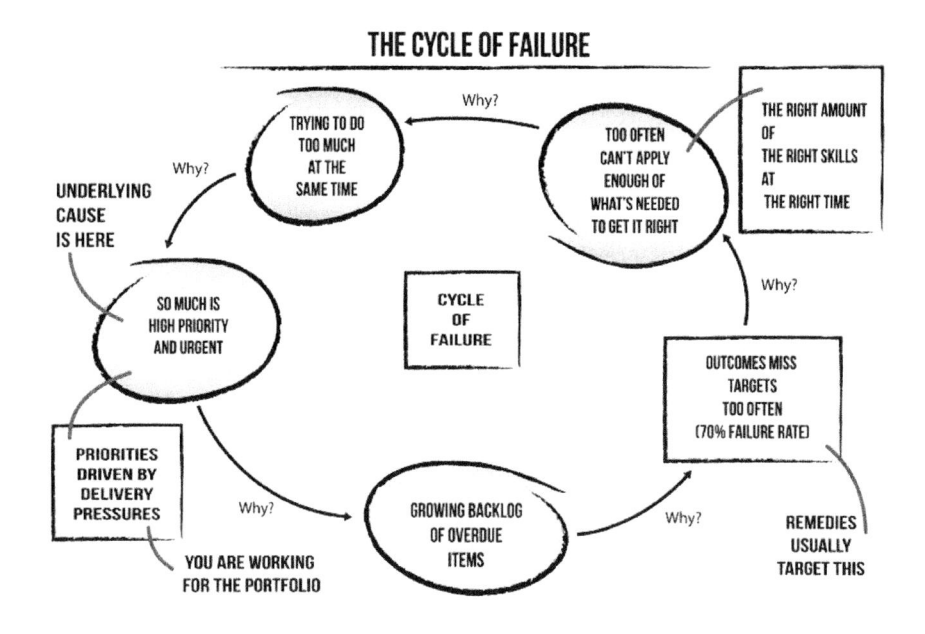

Figure 1: The cycle of failure

Hitting targets on cost, time, quality of output and enabling the expected return from the investment, is what projects and programmes need to do – getting projects right. (Selecting the right projects is covered in Chapter 4). Understandably therefore, in trying to break out of this cycle the focus has been on improving project and programme delivery.

The problem with this approach is that to hit targets requires the workload to be at a manageable level, which can only be maintained if targets are hit. It's Catch 22. Trying to hit targets without addressing the workload clearly doesn't work – witness the persistent 70% failure rate. Therefore, to continue to address the symptoms and not the underlying cause – trying to do too much – will keep you perpetually missing targets.

There is certainly room for improvement in the delivery of projects and programmes, and every effort should be made to continue to address that shortfall, because without effective management at that level the portfolio will not function. Conversely, improvements at the project and programme level won't fully bear fruit whilst the underlying cause remains unaddressed. Fix the problem at the portfolio level and you'll see a huge increase in value coming from the measures aimed at improving project and programme delivery performance.

There are of course success stories – the 30%. These tend to have a better track record because they get the resources, in its broadest sense, that they need to deliver, and many of them are too small and too quick to be at high risk of suffering damage. If all projects and programmes got the resources and the backing they needed – the right amount of the right skill at the right time – the failure rate would drop sharply. But there's a limit to what can be provided. Determining that limit will enable the workload to be made manageable.

It stops you exploiting synergies

Synergies are a very simple yet highly effective way of getting more from less – something every organisation should be striving to achieve from every operation it runs. Change is a means by which this can be readily exploited, but it requires a holistic approach. However, as most organisations think of change as projects and programmes, rather than portfolios, the current approach is predicated on initiatives being shaped and delivered independently from each other. This stops synergies being identified and exploited. These synergies can come from initiatives complementing each other, from turning conflicting priorities into mutually beneficial ones, and by addressing several apparently disparate requirements with one solution that benefits all. Identifying and exploiting these can only come from treating the investment as holistic and joined-up, not a collection of silos, and embedding them in portfolio planning (Chapter 4). But this won't happen without a shift in perspective. Therefore, to address the underlying cause of failure and exploit the potential for added value that a holistic approach would bring, a change in mindset is required.

Chapter summary

The current approach to project and programme delivery won't let you get change working for you:

- Too many targets continue to be missed too often.
- The remedies to address this are targeted at the symptoms – project and programme delivery, rather than the underlying cause – ineffective portfolio management.
- The portfolio management problem is constantly trying to do more than you have capacity for.
- Therefore, continuing to tackle the symptoms and not the workload traps you in a cycle of failure.
- And by not applying portfolio management principles you also miss out on exploiting synergies.
- So, you need to change your approach, or you risk staying trapped, and the key to unlocking that is a shift in mindset. Mindset pre-requisites are covered next.

3: Mindset pre-requisites for changing approach

There are seven aspects to this, the 'magnificent seven' if you like:

1. Understand and embrace the principles and benefits of 'genuine' portfolio management.

2. Regard the leadership as one governing team for 'one' organisation, not a collection of senior managers whose primary concern is their own patch – there's no room for silos or parochial self-interest.

3. Embrace change as the investment in the future of the organisation and an integral part of day-to-day business, forget 'business as usual' versus 'Change', it's all 'business as usual'.

4. Recognise the need to 'spring clean' all year round – be constantly ready to dispense with practices, projects and programmes that are no longer of value and embrace new ones that are. Critical amongst the new practices is portfolio management.

5. Acknowledge that change cannot be given effect without the efforts of people working collaboratively, both those 'giving' and those 'receiving'. They must be engaged and supported in their endeavours throughout.

6. Cherish 'small is beautiful', it's nimbler and pays back faster. Keep adding value with smaller, more frequent releases that, like some of the 30%, are easier to accommodate and provide greater flexibility in shaping the investment. They also foster positive organisational energy by establishing a momentum of regular achievement.

7. Adopt a sense of urgency – procrastination is the enemy of change, and therefore of your organisation's future prosperity. 'How can we make it happen?' rather than 'reasons not to try' should be the driver.

The principles of portfolio management

Too many instances described as portfolio management are no more than management of a list of projects and programmes. Calling oversight of a list 'portfolio management' does not automatically apply the disciplines needed to run a portfolio, nor exploit the advantages that a holistic approach to the investment offers. Genuine portfolio management is about harnessing the investment as a whole, to drive maximum value from limited resources by balancing demand with supply and exploiting opportunities for synergies.

To emphasise the difference it brings, I use an air travel analogy to describe the positive effect on delivery, and a simple equation to illustrate the potential for even greater value to be gained from exploiting synergies.

Air Traffic Control

Imagine projects as single flights from A to B, and programmes as journeys requiring several flights (some concurrent and some sequential); portfolio management is air traffic control. Imagine what air travel would be like without air traffic control and you may begin to understand how much risk projects and programmes are exposed to without effective portfolio management in place.

Improving flights and journeys (projects and programmes) is certainly an ongoing requirement, but however good the aircraft, pilots, cabin crew and ground crew are, without air traffic control looking after runways and flight paths, taking off and arriving safely remains a very high-risk undertaking.

Air traffic control (portfolio management) addresses the natural imbalance between demand and supply and highlights opportunities for synergies. The aspects of supply that are implicated here are those that have the lowest capacity for throughput compared to other steps in the end-to-end delivery process. These are bottlenecks. Understanding them is critical to addressing the imbalance, or there is a risk that the wrong areas will be tackled, the imbalance left in place and the underlying cause of the problem left to continue. How to tackle this is covered in Chapter 4.

The power of six

Amongst your projects and programmes are likely to be some that don't sit quite neatly in alignment with each other, such as a major cost reduction at the same time as a need for heavy investment in digitalisation. Run as separate initiatives each potentially could reduce the impact and the value of the other because of the apparently competing objectives. There will be others where there is a synergy between them that if exploited would not only enable the initiatives to be delivered successfully and produce the expected returns, but the effects of the synergy could add even more value, financial or otherwise, to your portfolio outcomes. You may well find that conflicting initiatives can be turned into synergistic ones. But this opportunity will be missed if the programmes are sponsored and run independently of each other.

Identifying the potential negatives and embracing the potential positive combinations can make a significant difference to the value of your portfolio. This can be illustrated using the example mentioned above and based on a real situation. A major cost reduction programme and a heavy investment in technology to digitalise the customer service offering were running concurrently but sponsored separately and had diametrically opposing requirements relating to expense. Without addressing this conflict, the cost reduction programme was struggling to meet its targets as the digital programme was increasing expense to achieve its own aims. But its aims in turn were thwarted because of the restrictions on expense imposed by the cost reduction programme. In this example, the divisive approach meant the outcome would equate to 2+2=1. In other words, the outcome was worse than if one programme had been allowed to deliver successfully – in effect they undermined each other. If the programmes had not had conflicting objectives and both delivered successfully, then the outcome would have been 2+2=4. A good result.

However, by making the digital programme the means by which additional cost would be taken out of the operation through automation, and the cost out programme removing some unnecessary and costly legacy processes that would otherwise have compromised the outcomes of the digital programme, both delivered successfully with greater returns than if run separately. The conflicting priorities were turned into mutual support, enhancing the value of each of them, which meant in each case '2' became '3'. With the benefit of air traffic control keeping them both safe the overall outcome was therefore 2+2=6. This is not only providing additional value, but in doing so adding to the organisation's strength in pursuit of its ambitions. Hence the 'power of six'.

Synergy may also come from enabling apparently disparate requirements to be combined in a way that allows them all to be successfully addressed through one investment rather than a separate investment for each one. These are often, but not exclusively, found in generic business operating processes such as reporting tools or document management systems. Using the air travel analogy this is like finding three airlines trying to make the same journey at the same time to the same destination with the same type of cargo and the same outcome in mind. Combining these into one flight reduces cost (one flight instead of three), time (you don't have to queue so much for take-off, flight paths and landing) and risk (there are two fewer journeys taking place at the same time on the same flight path). You get there safer, quicker and at lower cost – three into one is a winner for all. Using this example, you only need to find a couple of opportunities to combine initiatives on a 1 for 3 basis and you have an equation equivalent to 1+1=6.

Yes, the mathematics might sound simplistic, but the point is valid even if the stats can be argued: Portfolio management unleashes the potential of synergies to add much more value than you would get from running projects and programmes in silos. In the examples above, to the tune of at least 50%, but probably a great deal more.

Air traffic control and the power of six together are a formidable weapon in making the portfolio work for you.

Top-down collective responsibility, not silos

The benefits described above won't come unless the organisation works collaboratively. Collaboration is the essence of portfolio management. Without it, you will remain trapped in the cycle of failure. This means the leadership team must act with a collective responsibility that outweighs that for which they are charged in the business units they lead. What's required is similar to the principles underpinning the structure of Government. The executive, in this case the Cabinet, is made up of Secretaries of State, each of whom have responsibilities relating to their brief, the Department they are appointed to run. But as the Cabinet they are required to act as a single governing body for the entire realm, not a collection of Secretaries of State operating independently. The principle is that Government is paramount to the individual departments, who take their direction from Government. (I stress that I'm basing this analogy on the principles regardless of the extent to which they are followed in practice). The organisation's leadership team must follow these principles if they are to get change working for them. They need to operate as one when forming the organisation's ambitions, selecting areas for investment then guiding and enabling it all to come to fruition. This is particularly important in the post COVID world, when having to lead all the operations in a transition to accommodate different working patterns that have suddenly been forced on them. Collaboration across the entire organisation will be critical in enabling the organisation to cope with this.

By working collaboratively, and commissioning change on a joined-up basis, commitments (psychological, contractual or otherwise) need not be made until it's clear there's a very good chance they can be honoured. In essence you get 'Ready, Aim, Fire', and not the other way around, which is too often where some leaders find themselves when change has been commissioned on a silo basis. Expectations of the 'Secretaries of State' in relation to their own contributions can therefore be more realistically set and aligned with what's achievable. This relieves tension and fosters a more collaborative rather than competitive atmosphere amongst the leadership team, which is then more readily able to permeate through the organisation.

It also eliminates the need for some leaders to sponsor 'hidden' portfolios that by-pass the formal arrangements because they believe it's the only way to get things done and meet their targets. In reality these cause untold damage to the ability of the organisation as a whole to progress. The existence of these 'hidden' arrangements is another symptom of failing portfolios.

Collaboration amongst the leadership is a vital pre-requisite for enabling the benefits of air traffic control and the power of six. Embedding this behaviour in the culture is covered in Chapter 5.

'Change' is 'Business as Usual'

The concept of 'change' versus 'business as usual' (BAU), sometimes referred to as 'run' or 'keep the lights on' (KTLO), emerged in the late 1980s when the volume of project activity began to increase, fuelled by growth in the use of technology, to the extent that some degree of control was needed over how much funding and resource was being devoted to it.

Consequently, the structure of budgets started to reflect what was required for 'BAU' and separately for 'change'. The notion being that 'change' was discretionary, and the first place where any 'give' might come from when money was tight. Thirty years on and the two are often still distinguished in the same way – 'BAU' regarded as the main day-to-day operation, stability and reliability, and 'change' as discretionary, innovative improvements. This view is often found in contemporary training material.

A good test of how this mindset prevails in an organisation is the extent to which change activity is 'parked' in times of crisis, such as the impact of COVID-19. Another is how much change activity is included in Business Continuity and Disaster Recovery Plans. It's usually conspicuous by its absence.

This suggests that for many organisations, when the going gets tough, 'change' is a luxury that can be sacrificed. This is tantamount to jeopardising the organisation's medium to long term future in order to address short-term crises.

Ironically, treating it in this way does have serious short-term implications as well. Whilst 'change' is not regarded as an integral part of the day-to-day 'real' business, it fosters a mindset of isolation amongst the 'change community' – a feeling of 'us and them'.

This isolation provokes a need for those in change to find another source of recognition and respect. It's a bit like a new member desperately trying to establish their credentials with an unwelcoming group they've just joined. They seek solace amongst those of a like-mind or a similar position for recognition and reward. In change this often emerges as a 'sub' culture, a paradigm even, developing a new 'specialism', with its own language, practices, theories, rules and conventions. This in turn generates feeder industries for training, certification, and 'expertise'. All of which have laudable intentions for enabling success, but this isolation brings a risk that they become self-serving, focussed on their own agenda, and as such setting themselves apart from the very thing they are for – to make organisations consistently successful.

So, organisations marginalise change at their peril. To be successful, change must be an integral part of the day-to-day operation and those involved regarded as vital to securing long-term success. Of course, there is a distinction between developing new aspects of operation alongside existing arrangements pending their adoption, and that this transition has to be carefully managed. But the critical nature of this transition emphasises why the two should be seen as integral, rather than as a handing over of the baton. Change *is* 'business as usual', 'business as usual' *is* continuous, innovative improvements. Change also acts as a sense check on whether ambitions are realistic. However attractive those ambitions might be, if you can't get the required changes in place, trying to pursue them is likely to end in failure.

Change is, and will be, a fundamental requirement of business just to survive, let alone prosper. Making the right investment and realising the return on it can be the difference between being a front runner, an also ran and a failure. As such, it should be a central part of an organisation's concerns.

Spring clean all year round

Resource is precious and expensive. Spring cleaning all year round makes sure that no resource (human or otherwise) is wasted on poor value activity. This includes projects and programmes as well as practices and processes that are no longer of value, however much may have been spent on them already. You can't un-spend what's spent but you can avoid wasting resources that haven't been spent yet. Staying on top of this will allow your portfolio to run much smoother and faster and enjoy the best returns sooner by spending every penny and every hour wisely.

Getting rid of projects and programmes that are no longer valid investments and embracing the most valuable possible instead comes in the approach to portfolio planning that is covered in Chapter 4. The new governance arrangements covered in Chapter 5 will ensure this stance remains in perpetuity.

In terms of practices and processes, many checks and balances that are in place to compensate for poor delivery can be dispensed with once the underlying cause of failure is addressed, as the rate of failure will plummet. These can be very expensive and time-consuming, so their loss will be a welcome relief to the organisation's resources. You may already recognise some as unwelcome bureaucracy. Each organisation will have its own idiosyncrasies in this respect, so you will need to decide for yourself what can be dispensed with. Chapter 5 contains a guide to help you weed out those killing value and liberate those that will add an awful lot more.

Beyond those, there is further advantage to be gained from applying the same principle to all operations – to strive to make every element of operations add value.

Only people make things happen

Change won't happen without people and the more fired up they are and motivated to make it work, the more you'll get from them in return. You know this already. You'll also find as you go through this book how vital they are in getting change to work for you, and how what you put in place can provide them with a thoroughly enjoyable and rewarding experience that will help them flourish and pay dividends for all concerned. When you consider how much knowledge, skill and experience they bring it makes sense for them to be active participants in shaping how change gets delivered. And for that participation to be collaborative so that the immense amount of knowledge, skill and experience can be shared for mutual benefit and accelerated learning. This will become apparent when modelling options for a balanced workload, covered in Chapter 4, and in shaping the team to support the ongoing investment in Chapter 5. The benefits of engagement and collaboration have long been reported. What I've found effective in supporting and motivating teams and individuals, always consists of the same basic ingredients – communication, listening, understanding, being understood and involvement. Conveniently these aspects can be encapsulated in an acronym – CLUB – that also has a collaborative sentiment.

Leadership has a vital role to play in all this. Ultimately, the role of a leader is to make others successful. As long as what's defined as success is in line with ambition, everyone will win as a result. You also know that it's easier to manage and develop people when you have enough time. Breaking free from the cycle of failure and turning into one of success will give you that time, which in turn will ensure you have a fully motivated and capable team to keep you perpetually successful. The section on growing capability in Chapter 5 covers the need for ongoing training and development, and how to make the most effective use of it.

The challenge is how to cope in the meantime, especially in the light of the impact COVID has had on working arrangements. Ironically, making the workforce remote and fragmented has meant that some less productive means of managing, like monitoring hours worked and presence in the office are no longer an easy option. Instead, focus has had to shift to output and outcomes. Rightly so, as these are what make the difference between succeeding and failing as a business. However, it's also thrown up the challenge of how physical isolation doesn't allow the benefits of co-location in communication and idea exchange on an informal, organic basis, let alone formal gatherings in brainstorming sessions. And of course, there's the psychological impact – solitary confinement is usually regarded as a punishment. In that sense leadership has been put to the test. Technology can help to some extent – virtual meetings are much easier than a few years ago – but the emotional well-being that comes with a mutual supportive community spirit is much harder to attain when people are not in close proximity. In that sense leadership has to find a way of emulating the benefits of a community, even when its members are isolated. There is some help with this, along with some team building techniques in Chapter 5.

Small is beautiful

There is certainly a modern trend towards smaller, more frequent deliveries as opposed to monolithic 'big bang' implementations of yesteryear, thanks to the drive to adopt agility in delivering change. However, there are still many large programmes that dominate the landscape and take months if not years before providing significant value. Of course, there will be the need for large undertakings such as the digitalisation of group-wide operations. However, all large-scale initiatives can be delivered in more than one way. The challenge is to find a way of enabling value to be delivered regularly, especially if it is not wasted regardless of what follows. There are significant benefits to this:

- The organisation starts getting a return on its investment sooner, which of course it can then reinvest – a bit like a housing developer releasing homes for sale and occupation before the entire site is complete.

- It enables flexibility in the shape of the portfolio, which is essential to keep things under control and take advantage of opportunities.

- It allows spring cleaning regularly. The psychological barrier to losing poor value initiatives yet to deliver but already having cost a fortune is much easier when what has been 'sunk' has already returned some value.

- It emulates some elements of the '30%'. Initiatives are more likely to succeed if they are smaller, less complex and able to fit more readily into the portfolio – it's one means of making the workload manageable.

This means enabling flexibility to accommodate changes driven by external or internal factors, realise faster returns and continued progress towards ambitions, all of which make the portfolio work for you.

Procrastination is the enemy of change

Procrastination is the enemy of change – they are mutually exclusive. Procrastination is resistance, and organisations that resist change will die, it's just a matter of time. Procrastination also comes in the form of shaping deliveries to delay the release of value, such as 'big bang' implementations. Adopting 'small is beautiful' will address this. But ultimately, the longer you take to make change work for you, the worse it will get.

Chapter summary

A shift in mindset is a pre-requisite for changing the approach from one that traps you in a cycle of failure to one that keeps you in a cycle of success. The key areas to embrace are the 'magnificent seven':

1. The principles and benefits of portfolio management, air traffic control and the power of six.
2. Top down collective responsibility, working together as one team not a collection of silos.
3. Change is 'business as usual'.
4. Spring clean all year round to keep resource on value adding, not value destroying activities.
5. Change will only happen through the efforts of people so 'CLUB' together.
6. Small is beautiful – keep a momentum of frequent, lower risk, value adding releases.
7. Procrastination is the enemy of change.

…So, let's get started…!

4: How to turn the cycle of failure into a cycle of success

Make the workload manageable

To make the organisational change workload manageable requires breaking the link between doing too much at the same time and the high volume of top priority and urgent projects and programmes that leads to this happening (see figure 2).

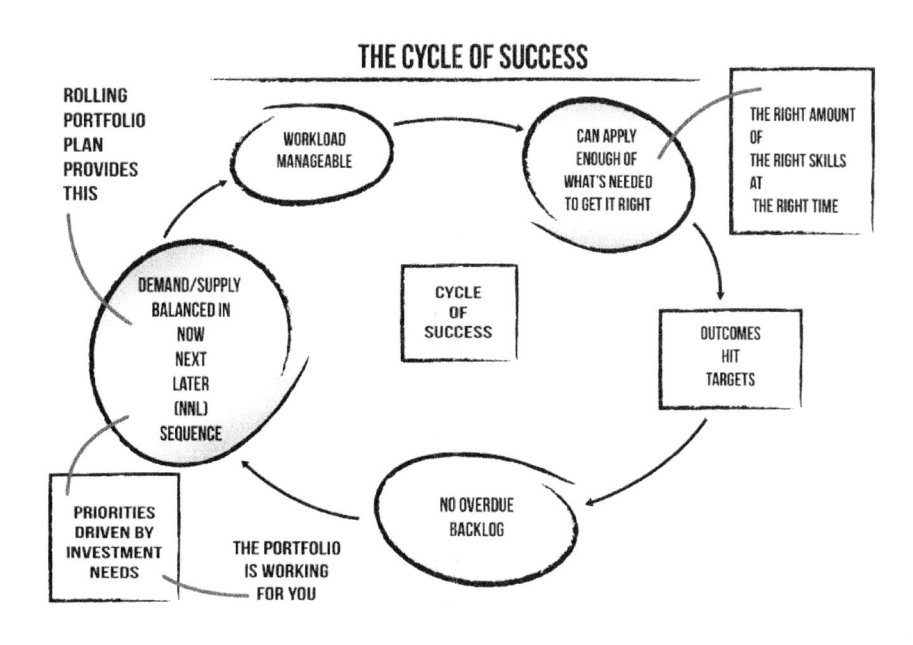

THE CYCLE OF SUCCESS

ROLLING PORTFOLIO PLAN PROVIDES THIS → WORKLOAD MANAGEABLE → CAN APPLY ENOUGH OF WHAT'S NEEDED TO GET IT RIGHT → THE RIGHT AMOUNT OF THE RIGHT SKILLS AT THE RIGHT TIME → OUTCOMES HIT TARGETS → NO OVERDUE BACKLOG → DEMAND/SUPPLY BALANCED IN NOW NEXT LATER (NNL) SEQUENCE → CYCLE OF SUCCESS

PRIORITIES DRIVEN BY INVESTMENT NEEDS

THE PORTFOLIO IS WORKING FOR YOU

Figure 2: The cycle of success

This requires a delivery plan based on a schedule of 'now, next, later' (NNL) priorities to replace the list of top priority, urgent project and programmes currently being used. An NNL prioritisation balances demand with supply whilst retaining alignment with ambition. Because the balance makes the workload manageable, there is enough time to apply the right amount of the right skill at the right time to get things right. This in turn means targets will get hit, which in turn eliminates the growing backlog of overdue projects and programmes. As a result, 'later' in this scenario is actually 'sooner' than it would have been in the free-for-all high priority bun fight associated with the current approach. And because targets are getting hit, a balanced workload can be maintained on an NNL basis, which means targets will continue to be hit. And so on. As such you turn the cycle of failure into a cycle of success and get to realise the return on your investment in line with ambition and expectation continually.

The cycle of success switches the emphasis from playing catch up with yesterday, to getting ahead of tomorrow because the priorities are driven by the value of investment returns rather than delivery pressures. You are now in control of your future and the portfolio is working for you, not you for the portfolio.

The NNL prioritisation is created and maintained by embedding the balance between demand for investment priorities with supply side constraints in a rolling portfolio plan. How to do this is covered in Chapter 4. To achieve this balance, both demand and supply need to be understood and quantified, because in organisational change these two are naturally at odds with each other:

- Demand can be very easily volatile – in volume, shape, size, complexity and frequency.

- Supply can be very easily inflexible. The lion's share of supply is usually the permanent workforce in the organisation. By its nature it cannot readily change shape, size, complexity, capability and frequency of availability. Other aspects of supply, such as the technical and physical estate are likewise not readily able to flex.

In reality, the volume of demand overall is constantly too high for the reasons cited earlier. The good news is that it can be readily reduced, as times of crisis have shown and as you will see when going through the new approach to building and maintaining a portfolio plan. The shape, size, complexity and frequency can quite easily be all over the place, but with intervention in the shape of a balanced plan can be made much more manageable.

Reducing volatility in demand is comparatively easier than trying to make supply more flexible. So, by working out the degree to which supply can flex, demand can then be shaped around it. This won't be an exact science and shouldn't be or you risk spending unnecessary time trying to get to a forensic level of detail that won't affect the decisions to be made. Ultimately, you need to establish a range within which demand and supply can balance with each other and cope with acceptable changes without the plan being derailed and supply becoming overwhelmed. This comes as part of modelling when building the portfolio plan.

Determine and support organisational constraints – Supply

The concept of bottlenecks in delivery of change

The capacity for throughput in any production system is never infinite, so at some point there must be a limit, a constraint, that needs to be respected. That constraint is a bottleneck. It is the point at which the capacity to cope with the work is lower than anywhere else in the end-to-end operation. Trying to do more than a bottleneck can cope with puts the whole operation at risk.

The concept of bottlenecks as operational risks is not new. This principle featured in the manufacturing process adopted by Toyota in its Toyota Production System of the 1930's to improve production performance and throughput by identifying and improving the system level bottlenecks. In *The Goal* published in 1984, Eliyahu M. Goldratt included the concept in the Theory of Constraints, which is based on the premise that a chain is no stronger than its weakest link. The theory of constraints is a management philosophy aimed at helping organisations continually achieve their goals. Goldratt (1997) adapted the concept to project management in his book *Critical Chain*.

The weakest link is the bottleneck, which determines the rate of throughput for the entire system. Imagine someone standing on a garden hose. However hard you turn on the tap and however big the sprinkler is, you will only get a trickle out of the end. The output from the hose is limited by the capacity at the point where someone is standing on it. Investing in a more powerful tap or a larger sprinkler is a waste until you address the bottleneck. Indeed, a more powerful tap is potentially dangerous given the increased pressure it would apply at the bottleneck.

This is no different to the experience of many people in an operational bottleneck. In the delivery of change they are normally some of the most critical resources in the end-to-end operation. They possess skills, knowledge, capability and authority that are in short supply (hence the narrower bandwidth). Despite this they are often put under immense pressure to maintain a higher volume of throughput than they can reasonably cope with, and to make sure their output is of the required quality for the next step to progress.

And it's not just about volume. Multi-tasking has its limits beyond which it reduces productivity and has an adverse effect on the cognitive ability of the multi-tasker. In effect it slows things down and lowers the quality of the output. There has been much research, publicly available, showing the impact of this, and the adverse effects on well-being and productivity are also covered in the Theory of Constraints Handbook, Cox and Schleier (2010). Many of those affected have an overloaded backlog of change and often a 'day job' as well. All this increases the risk that they will take longer to get things done or get them wrong or both. They are well aware of the consequences of being seen as an inhibiter of progress. And as specialists with highly regarded knowledge and expertise, they also have a reputation to protect.

As a result, they do what they can to cope, consequently many problems often don't emerge until later. By then it's much more time-consuming and expensive to put them right. This has a significant impact on individual initiatives, the rest of the portfolio and of course the people concerned.

Identify the scope of supply

Although some bottlenecks may seem fairly obvious, it's worth beginning with what the supply side consists of in totality. By this I mean all the 'inputs' required by the portfolio to get things commissioned, delivered and implemented into the day-to-day operation. This is so that you can then be sure you will have unearthed all the likely suspects that could impact throughput. I have found that while most bottlenecks are fairly obvious, there are sometimes a few surprises – some you thought would be bottlenecks turn out not to be and vice versa, hence the value in seeing the full scope before acting on assumptions. After completing this for the first time you'll only have to 'turn the handle' to keep it going.

Some of the inputs to change are obvious like project managers and business analysts, some may not be, and it is likely that the more obscure are where the bottleneck is. And bear in mind the operation receiving an implementation to assume into its day-to-day operation also has a capacity that will affect the rate of throughput, so that capacity must be included in this as well.

To identify the inputs, I use a simple approach based on a standard business process model – Inputs, Transformation Process and Outputs. That's it. The outputs are obviously the outcomes and associated value from the delivery and the transformation is the portfolio of programmes and projects. What's needed for this exercise is literally the inputs to the transformation. As an example, based on making tea for four, you may determine the inputs as: The original request, tea, milk, sugar, cups, saucers, spoons, teapot, tea strainer, kettle, one tea maker, and four tea drinkers. By virtue of a process using these ingredients you end up with the four tea drinkers being served tea by the tea maker.

To gather the information with the business process model, I suggest using brainstorming workshops with people who can readily identify all the inputs, their capacity, capability and dependencies. It doesn't matter what level in the hierarchy those involved are as long as they can come up with the answers, particularly the obscure ones. Start the brainstorming with 'brainwriting', to give people a few minutes to produce something unchallenged. Then I suggest using a 'gallery', where everyone posts up their ideas and wanders around the room to share and inspire others to add to them.

If ideas dry up too early, try an idea-generating technique called 'reversal'. This is a form of brainstorming that asks the opposite of what you are trying to come up with. For example, "if we want stuff to fail, who or what should we leave out?", which by contrast tells you that it's needed to succeed, so include it.

This is the approach that works for me. An alternative method such as systems mapping can be just as effective. It helps define the organisation as a system by simply mapping its components, how they link together and relate to other components beyond the organisation's boundary. As long as you get what you need and the 'buy-in' of those affected, the approach doesn't really matter.

Because you're involving those 'in the thick of it', it shouldn't take long at all to come up with the answers. And it is amazing what you do come up with sometimes. In one place, this exercise highlighted the extraordinary number of third parties that were relied upon to help deliver, and how ripe that landscape was for rationalisation. Below are examples of the categories you are likely to come up with.

- People – this includes all those inside and outside the organisation involved in the end-to-end process – 'change' people, SMEs in business lines, those 'receiving' the implementation in the operation, and external organisations etc.

- Technology – the estate (especially the 'legacy'), applications platforms, the network, security, other aspects of the infrastructure, upgrade paths, compatibility, scaling, capability etc.

- Data – availability and integrity.

- The physical estate – buildings, equipment, training facilities, office accommodation, infrastructure. (I once worked in a relatively new development whilst further building work continued and regular interruption to the utilities' services had to be factored into implementation schedules).

- Policies and practices – formal and informal rules and frameworks, including regulatory and legal requirements, the extent of approvals required, how many stages (and for what purpose) there are in an end-to-end process.

- Finances – how have internal budgets enabled or restricted resource availability on internal expense; what restrictions and commitments are there on external expenses.

Ideally, you have a reliable and easy-to-use resource management system that will make data capture and modelling easier to manage, especially with scenario analysis when balancing demand and supply. If you don't, it's worth installing one. It doesn't need to be a top of the range platform costing a fortune, but just enough to suit your circumstances and provide what you need for the foreseeable future. SharePoint has worked for some, though it's not so easy for modelling large-scale scenarios. In keeping with the sentiments expressed so far, you need to make sure that whatever you use, you have the capacity and the capability to make it work for you. Solving one problem only to create two more is to be avoided. There is help on this towards the end of Chapter 5.

Find the bottlenecks and the limits to what they can cope with

Having identified the scope of supply you now need to home in on the bottlenecks. By definition there will be at least one, though it is unlikely there will be more than a handful. It is critical that you undertake this exercise and resist the temptation to jump straight to augmenting the delivery teams (with, for example, additional project managers or business analysts and IT skills) or you risk wasting time and money addressing something that isn't a bottleneck and as a result make the problem worse. Homing in on the bottlenecks will serve two purposes:

- To make sure the capacity of each bottleneck is respected when demand for it is aggregated in a portfolio plan.

- To understand the feasibility and extent of a potential increase in its bandwidth.

This will define the capacity around which you need to shape demand. The information you need about them is their identity, capacity, capability and dependencies, and what risks they are exposed to. To help you, the table below provides an illustration of what this might look like.

Table 1: Bottleneck attributes

Attribute	Description
Identity	Who or what and where are they? Personnel, equipment, inside or outside the organisation.
Capacity	How much is available? When, amount of effort, duration – this is the nub of the constraint. I suggest this is quantified in the same way you plan, estimate and report, e.g.: in 'days', or hours, or 'full time equivalent (FTE)' for people. You will need a clear and consistently used definition of an FTE here or you will run into difficulty.

	Duration in calendar terms – dates 'from' and 'to'.

You should also identify any circumstances that affect where the bottleneck might be. For example, whether the bottleneck is different in August because of the holiday season. Monitoring bottlenecks is therefore ongoing not a one-off exercise. |
| Capability | What is it that's in short supply? Skill set, experience, knowledge, facilities, authority etc.

Below are a few examples of the circumstances that might give rise to pressure on capability, I'm sure you can come up with many more:
- A major transformation programme, when you're used to running small to medium sized internal IT projects.
- The acquisition of a new technical platform, requiring skills and knowledge you haven't used before, so some are 'learning on the job' and can't cope with the same volume as more experienced practitioners.
- Third party suppliers rolling out a new product and doing likewise with several other customers at the same time.
- A major corporate activity has required a shift in the way the organisation operates, and any new deliveries are now subject to approval processes that are still being 'bedded in'. |
| Dependencies | Ingoing and outgoing dependencies; where to and where from, and potential conflicts in logical sequences.

These are dependencies at the portfolio level, that 'air traffic control' will need to manage to |

ensure smooth travel and safe arrival, on time with the right 'cargo'.

Whilst projects and programmes will have their own dependencies, the portfolio is interested in those that connect projects and programmes to each other. Some of these may be readily apparent, others may not until you start to unearth where they compete for shared resource, or when applying the power of six.

A common example here is subject matter expertise and professional specialisms (such as legal advice). As such, these have an influence on the shaping of the portfolio plan and may require a compromise on priorities in order to accommodate initiatives alongside each other. For example, the limit to what legal advice is available at any one time may affect the flow of regulatory programmes.

Somewhat different, but just as common is a legacy technical platform that has over the years grown to become the hub of the entire applications network. As such, all new applications have to 'register' their presence and establish communication with it. It means making changes to the platform and then involving it in the testing.

Not only is it a potential bottleneck, but because it is constantly being updated, air traffic control will need to help manage the sequence of those updates. Some updates may need others to have taken place before them in order to be able to continue safely. Project and programme 'assumptions' are a useful source of information here, provided of course that they have been declared and are available.

Risks	Obviously as bottlenecks, there is by definition already a risk identified. This point is about understanding whether there are any other 'threats' to take account of. For example, organisation changes that might affect capacity or capability in an already vulnerable area. Or to make an area vulnerable that at present is not a bottleneck.

There are a couple of other points to bear in mind:

- When assessing any potential third-party potential suppliers, required to help delivery of projects, programmes or portfolio management, apart from understanding where they are in the maturity of the product and service you're interested in, find out how active they are. For example, a small to medium sized supplier trying to get a new platform established is likely to be pouring resource into signing up significant numbers of new customers. This might be the same resource you will be relying on to support your implementation, so you might find this service becomes a bottleneck.

- Other corporate support functions will also need to contribute. For example, there may be legal, compliance, risk, HR, and audit issues that need to be taken into account when shaping the portfolio. These resources might be scarce and as such constrain some aspects of the ambition, the investments required and how they fit together in the portfolio plan.

Much of the information you need should already exist, it's just a case of getting your hands on it and pulling it together. Useful sources of information include:

- The output from the workshop exercise to identify the supply side inputs.

- First-hand experience from those involved.

- Project and programme assumptions, risk assessments and issues logs that regularly point to the same areas as being vulnerable.

- Places where measures have been added to compensate for and protect 'weak spots', such as selective 'ring-fencing' of some resource or additional checks and balances acting as a safety net.

- Any recent audits or programme and project reviews and 'lessons learned' or similar reports that may have highlighted areas of vulnerability.

You need enough information to see where capacity might run into difficulty and to judge the feasibility of making improvements to increase the bandwidth. Using the tea making example, if say the teapot has capacity for three cups only, then however much water you boil and tea you have, you won't be able to provide more than three cups at a time. So, you either have to get a bigger teapot or manage the throughput and expectations on the basis that three is the production limit.

In this example, it might be relatively easy to expand that particular bottleneck – the teapot. For others, it might be impractical at least in the short term. Increasing the number of test environments, or the number of subject matter experts with a deep understanding of one area of the organisation won't happen overnight. And, if you do make improvements in one area, it means you will by consequence make another area the bottleneck, so you need to make sure the adjustments are planned, and the sequence of making them is logical or you'll end up playing 'whack-a-mole' (the futile task of continually solving one problem only for another one to appear elsewhere). The following is a simple example to illustrate the sort of information you will be looking for:

Table 2: Bottleneck examples

Identity	Capacity	Capability	Dependencies
Model Office	4 full time testers available:	Current platform only and small-	In: Production-ready application suite with signed

Testing team in IT	Jul-Aug only 50% (2xFTE); Feb-Nov only 20% (1x FTE)	medium sized low complexity changes	off test plan and scripts 4 weeks in advance Out: Final implementation and handover
Legacy platform	Only changes from one initiative can be applied at any one time and they have to be proven before the platform is released for further 'upgrade'.	Changes must conform to the structure, format and technical configuration. Where they don't interfaces have to be built between the new application and the platform.	In: Fully detailed specification of changes scheduled one month in advance. Out: Fully tested and approved for release back into the live environment.

Having identified the bottlenecks and the details of their constraints in relation to capacity, capability and dependency, the next step is to protect them by making sure that:

- Their limits are respected.
- Any adjustments that can be made to increase those limits are considered.
- Any inputs to them are of the required quality so that they can be readily processed.
- Lower priority tasks do not get in the way.

This will form part of portfolio planning, when demand is shaped around the limits supply can cope with. Defining demand is next.

Define and manage organisational ambitions – Demand

Demand is derived from answering two basic questions about the organisation's future:

- What are we trying to achieve?
- Where do we need to invest?

Organisations that don't constantly ask themselves these two questions risk wandering aimlessly, wasting valuable resources and frustrating their stakeholders in the process. With an aimless approach the organisation is doomed, unless blessed with some abundance of good luck in the guise of a miracle.

To shape demand by answering these questions, it will help to have some facilitation and support available. This may come from whatever is currently in place to help with strategy and planning, including a programme or project management office (PMO). As you will come to see further on, there is a recommended facility to look after this as an integral part of the ongoing running of the investment portfolio, but it is assumed you won't have it in place the first time you try this new approach. In that case, using whatever is available that is closest with some external help will suffice whilst you put the new arrangements in place. The details are in Chapter 5 and can be used as a guide in the interim, especially to make sure that if you do seek external help, you get what you need.

What are we trying to achieve?

This is about clarifying the ambition, the means by which it will be achieved and what the organisation needs in order to make a success of pursuing it. It is encapsulated in the organisation's purpose, goals, and strategy.

The purpose is the reason for the organisation's existence. It often appears in mission statements as the impact the organisation intends to have on the lives of people and other organisations. Goals are, perhaps obviously, the specific targets the organisation has set itself over a specific period of time. These are usually quantifiable, such as profit levels, market share, market presence, share price, and service levels to name a few.

Obviously, purpose and goals should be aligned. Both reflect ambition. The next question is how to get there. That is strategy. Let's first clarify what is meant by strategy and therefore be more assured that it can be aligned with purpose and goals, and that the investment in change can support all three.

There are several definitions of strategy. The one I use is "The pattern of activities that is followed by an organisation in pursuit of its purpose". This implies that all its activities are in some way part of a strategy, whether consciously intended or not. Strategy doesn't have to be a planned, multi-year campaign encapsulated in reams of Word and PowerPoint. Henry Mintzberg, (1978) defined strategy as a pattern in a stream of decisions, which contrasts with the view of strategy as the product of planning. In that sense every organisation has a strategy even if it doesn't recognise it.

This means that firstly, the purpose must be clear or there's a huge risk you'll be investing in the wrong areas. And secondly, the goals and all the activities leading to them need to be aligned with the purpose or they are at best not going to help, and at worst may actively work against achieving that ambition. In either case you would be wasting valuable resource. Defining strategy in this way therefore enables a check on whether everything the organisation is doing is geared towards its ambition. Anything that isn't needs to be dispensed with, adjusted or the ambition must be modified. In any case, you need to be clear what your strategy is, and in relation to achieving success, what it needs to be. Ideally, those two are the same, or some refinement will be needed.

There are a couple of other points to make about strategy. It is not 'To be number 1 in the marketplace'. This is a goal. Strategy is what you do to get there. It is not long term only. It is short, medium and long term. Sometimes 'tactical' is used to excuse some 'short-term' activity that appears to be at odds with 'the strategy'.

So, strategy is how you pursue your ambitions. This in turn should clarify what you need to help you do just that, and consequently where you need to invest in capability. This investment becomes your change portfolio. To illustrate the connection between these, an example based on a fictitious financial services company is below:

Table 3: Example, 'what are we trying to achieve?'

Money Tree Ltd ambitions			
Purpose	**Goal**	**Strategy**	**Capability needed**
To help people	To become the number one	A mix of differentiation	M&A expertise.

achieve long-term financial security before and during retirement.	savings, investments and personal pensions provider in the UK by 2025, with a turnover in excess of £10bn p.a. and a cost base reduction of 10% each year till then.	and cost focus: Divest interests in non-profit making markets; acquire niche expertise in the UK market. Target the middle-income bracket where there is most growth potential. Implement a self-service digital platform for retail customers for faster and cheaper operational process times.	Data and digital platform integration. Digital marketing. Regulatory compliance. Operations integration. Major programme delivery.

In this example Money Tree Ltd has decided that in order to fulfil its purpose and be a success it must become the leading player in the UK market within five years, measured by a turnover in excess of £10bn. In order to do that it is rationalising its business to focus more on the UK market, where it sees the most growth potential especially in the middle-income segment, and enhance its capability by acquiring some niche expertise in certain aspects of the supply chain, as opposed to trying to grow its own. Having recognised the capability required to achieve all this it can then determine the areas requiring investment.

Where do we need to invest?

This investment is required to strengthen the organisation so that it can pursue its strategy and achieve its ambitions.

WHERE DO WE NEED TO INVEST?

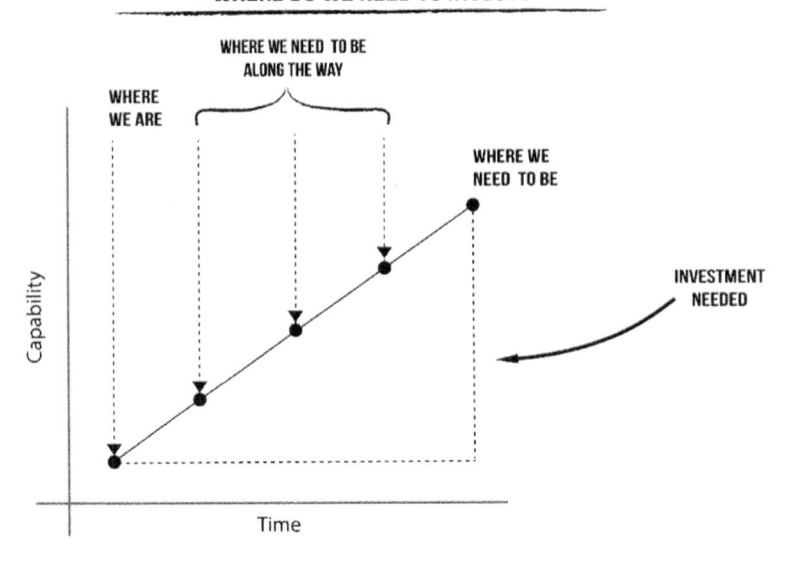

Figure 3: Where do we need to invest?

You will need the outcome of a gap analysis showing the organisation's current capability compared to what it requires in order to progress. Some, ideally all, of this information should be readily available. Often it comes from a strategic review. In any case, you need to be clear about the areas to be targeted and how. In some cases, this might be through organic growth, in others via acquisition of the capability from external sources.

If the information is not readily available and you need to conduct a gap analysis, there are plenty of management tools in place to help. Table 4, below, contains reference to some that I use in strategy development and undoubtedly are familiar to you. There is an important point here. If there is lack of clarity about ambition, strategy and what's required to pursue it, there's a high risk of investing in the wrong areas.

Table 4: Example management tools for 'where do we need to invest?'

Tool	How it helps
SWOT – **S**trengths, **W**eaknesses, **O**pportunities, **T**hreats	As I'm sure you know, SW are internal capabilities for coping with the external, OT, challenges. Using

	this in the context of the ambition will help direct investment to the right places.
STEEPL (or variations thereof) – **S**ocial, **T**echnical, **E**conomical, **E**nvironmental, **P**olitical, **L**egal.	This external view can help identify where **O**pportunities and **T**hreats might come from.
Porter's 5 forces (1979)	Another external view assessing the dynamics of the market the organisation is operating or potentially operating in and hence where **O**pportunities and **T**hreats might come from, and where strengths can be exploited, or weaknesses expose vulnerability.
Porter's Value Chain (1985)	It maps out the organisation as a system of inputs, transformation processes and outputs adding value along the way to produce quality goods and services. It is a useful tool in strategy development and as such in shaping where investment is required.

Prioritising investment areas

As well as determining the areas for investment, the leadership in the guise of a 'Cabinet' should agree which of them are the most important based on what's best for the organisation in pursuit of its ambitions. This is where a spirit of collaboration is vital. If anyone tries to grab and hold onto what they can at the expense of their colleagues, and by implication, the organisation, it will cause unnecessary delay and put the whole portfolio and consequently the organisation's future at risk. Working in silos at this stage makes it highly likely that at least psychological if not contractual commitments will be made that can't be honoured, but nor can they be readily dispensed with. There may well be many great candidates for investment, but there will never be room for everything, so it is critical to agree collectively where the priorities lie.

The priorities must be driven by the value of outcomes, any timing requirements, and whether there are any dependencies between them. The point about dependencies is very important. One of the key benefits of managing a portfolio rather than a list of projects and programmes is how these dependencies are managed to add value. There are two types of dependency to consider when prioritising at the portfolio level:

The logical dependency

This is when something has to be preceded by something else or it won't work. For example, programme A has to complete an upgrade to a central IT platform, because without it programme B cannot deliver its new digital offering. Programme B has planned on the assumption (declared or not) that the upgrade will have taken place.

The investment dependency – the power of six

Chapter 3 introduced the portfolio principle of 'the power of six'. It should be applied here to avoid potential conflicts, and to look for complementary investments that can have a mutually beneficial impact. The need to balance demand with supply is paramount, so must be respected when looking for synergies between the investments, but the advantage that can be gained from them must be exploited or the opportunity for even greater value will be missed. Looking for opportunities to get 6 from 2+2, or 1+1 when combining requirements into singular investments, as mentioned before, should in any case be a pursuit that the leadership is preoccupied with across the whole organisation – getting more from less.

The search for this extra value should also foster a spirit of collaboration amongst the leadership, which in turn means more of the portfolio can produce 6 more regularly, which in turn means you are likely to get more collaboration from the leadership – it's self-perpetuating.

By agreeing the investment priorities and power of six opportunities collaboratively at this stage, the projects and programmes contributing will automatically attain the priority associated with the investment, be shaped by the power of six and complement each other as a holistic investment.

A worked example

Using the Money Tree example to illustrate where investment considerations sit in relation to ambition, the table below shows it needs to invest in business rationalisation (divesting, acquiring and integrating), a new digital platform for the customer service offering, and regulatory compliance. It must also ensure that its programme delivery capability can cope. The conversion from manual to digital customer service will also require rationalising the supporting operations businesses. As such you'd expect to see all these featuring prominently in the investment portfolio. In terms of how the these are prioritised, the value, timing and dependencies (both logical and the power of six) tests should be used. In this example, it might mean that the business restructure is a pre-requisite for the acquisition integration, likewise the digital platform for data integration. Applying the power of six might show how the cost reduction initiative and the digital platform can mutually benefit each other.

Table 5: Example, 'where do we need to invest?'

Money Tree Ltd investment needed to enable ambitions to be met				
Purpose	**Goal**	**Strategy**	**Capability**	**Investment**
To help people achieve long-term financial security before and during retirement	To become the number one savings, and investments provider in the UK by 2025, with a turnover in excess of £10bn p.a. and a cost base reduction of 10% each	Divest interests in non-profit making markets; acquire niche expertise in the UK market. Target the middle-income bracket where there is most	M&A expertise. Data and digital platform integration. Digital marketing. Regulatory compliance. Operations integration. Major programme delivery.	Business restructure; acquisition integration; Digital platform; data integration; business divestment; Regulatory compliance; Cost reduction initiative

| | year till then. | growth potential. Implement a self-service digital platform for retail customers for faster and cheaper operational process times. | | |

In shaping the required investment, Money Tree may find that its capability and capacity to change in the way required is beyond what it can cope with. For example, it doesn't have sufficient expertise and technical capability to implement quickly a new digital platform. In this case it either has to improve its capability rapidly or adjust its ambitions. The alternative is to plough ahead anyway and then run into difficulty causing irreparable damage to its performance and reputation.

This is a reminder of how change is the glue that holds together purpose, goals, strategy and operations. It also highlights how change is tasked with safeguarding two effects – to put new arrangements in place and to keep growing the organisation's capability to do so.

PURPOSE, GOALS, STRATEGY, OPERATIONS HELD TOGETHER BY CHANGE

AMBITIONS

PURPOSE
The intended impact on the lives of people and other organisations

GOALS
Targets to meet to fulfil purpose

STRATEGY
The pattern of activities followed in pursuit of its purpose and goals

OPERATIONS
The capability, competences, activities, culture, organisation required to succeed

THE MEANS BY WHICH THEY ARE ACHIEVED

INVESTMENT IN CHANGE

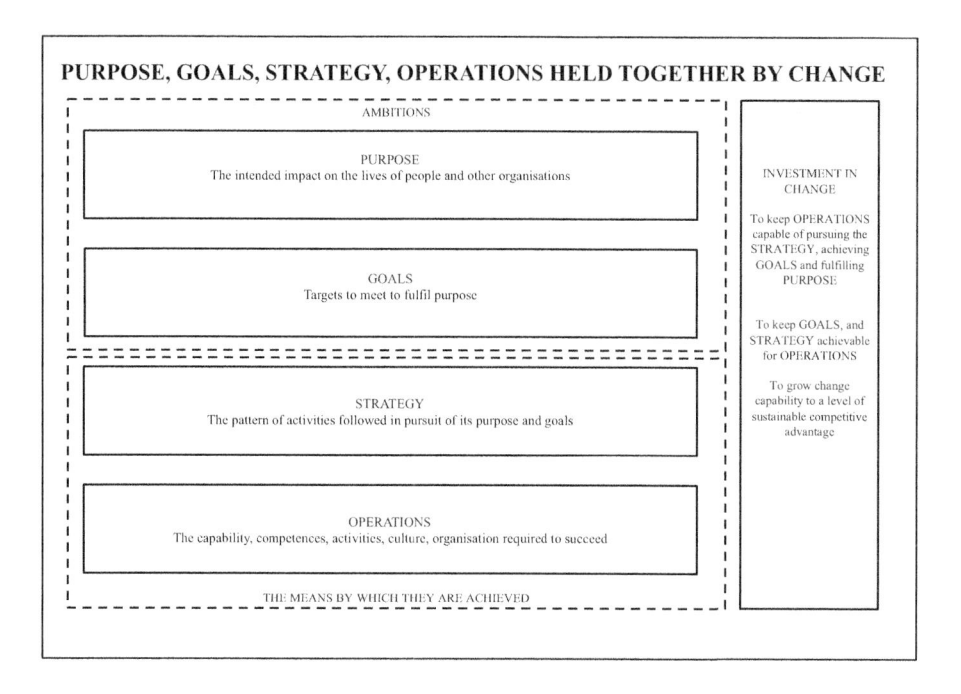

To keep OPERATIONS capable of pursuing the STRATEGY, achieving GOALS and fulfilling PURPOSE

To keep GOALS, and STRATEGY achievable for OPERATIONS

To grow change capability to a level of sustainable competitive advantage

Figure 4: Change is the glue keeping ambitions and investment in line

Criteria for investment appraisal

Determining the areas for investment is one thing, but to complete the definition of demand a bit more detail is required to clarify exactly how initiatives will contribute and what they require in order to do so. Initiatives won't actually make the cut until they have passed the alignment test and shown that they can fit within the supply side constraints when scheduled alongside others. So, the scrutiny is actually in two steps – firstly, whether there is a compelling business case in terms of the value it adds towards achievement of the organisation's ambitions, and secondly how well the delivery vehicle fits alongside others. Ideally the latter shows where there is benefit from applying the power of six.

The traditional method for projects and programmes to address these questions at this stage is with a business case and a high-level plan. Where they have already been produced then they can be used, provided of course they contain sufficient information to answer the questions. You need evidence of:

- Whether an initiative supports ambition and is worthy of consideration.

- How it would fit alongside others in a schedule when balancing demand with supply.

- To what extent it can be broken down into smaller, frequent value-adding releases.

Answering the following questions will provide the evidence. If any of it is missing, there is a risk that you will produce a plan with decision-changing gaps in it. Using a standard template will make it easier to collate the responses:

1. What is the outcome expected and how does this contribute to ambition? (This will automatically apply a priority to it by virtue of its association with the investment requirement already prioritised).

2. What resources (the supply side items from the previous exercise) at a high level are required to get this done?
    a. Human (specify skills, knowledge etc.), technical, physical, third-party resource.
    b. Pattern of usage – what is the level of demand for these resources throughout?
    c. Time frame – how long will it take, when is the outcome required?

3. Are there any dependencies between this and other initiatives, if so what?

4. Are there any assumptions that might affect the plans if they are wrong?

5. What delivery constraints, other than bottlenecks, such as legal or contractual deadlines is it subject to?

6. What level of risk does it pose, during execution and post implementation?

7. What are the implications of doing it (e.g. opportunity cost) or not doing it (e.g. exposure)?

8. How much will it cost (use a range) and what roughly is the external / internal cost ratio?

9. What levels of contingency are included, and for what specifically? This is discussed below.

10. How can the implementation strategy allow for smaller, more frequent releases of value-adding assets – what delivery options are there and can critical success factors be readily defined for them?

This list is not exhaustive. If there's anything that would help that is not on the list, then please add it. Together with the above you will need a high-level plan for each initiative. For new initiatives, this might be sketchy, and some assumptions will have to be made. This is no different to what should in any case be required to understand whether the initiative is a worthwhile concern.

The point to bear in mind here is that this information is needed to make the portfolio and the constituent projects and programmes as safe as they can be when scheduling them in the portfolio plan. The best examples of these 'brief' business cases are covered in two pages and take no more than a few hours to complete. These statements should be signed-off by the Executive responsible for the business area that is commissioning the investment. The governance framework needed to support the investment (Chapter 5) must enable appropriate scrutiny of the business cases.

For cross-business investments, a joint statement will be required. Use common sense to determine whether there should be primary and secondary 'partners' – whatever works best for the organisation, which ultimately is the test that should be applied at every stage. The collaborative approach that has got you this far means this shouldn't be such an issue as it is in a silo approach.

Control the use of contingency

Question 9 is about contingency. There's an important portfolio point to deal with here. Contingency is one of the approaches to mitigating risk. It's used extensively, sometimes without much scrutiny despite it commandeering a hefty chunk of resource. When it comes to fitting everything together, subsequently keeping it all safe, and making sure every penny is spent wisely, it is important to know what levels of contingency have been built in, why and for what purpose. Some of it may not have been 'consciously' added in.

Poorly managed contingency can ruin the health of a portfolio by denying access to vital resource and using it on the wrong problems, in many cases camouflaging them in the process. Well managed contingency is a boon to effective portfolio management – keeping things going in times of difficulty.

Unfortunately, there is a tendency for it to be used more as a safety net for those estimating and executing than for the organisation in dealing with variations from plan. And by the time it gets to final sign-off, the contingency in total is probably several times what at the outset would have been judged reasonable – each aggregation of estimates adding a bit more along the way. Whilst this is understandable given the history of delivery, bad use of contingency is tying up valuable resource unnecessarily and too readily being used in the wrong places.

In the current approach it is difficult to eke out what's hidden in layer upon layer of estimating. However, as the new approach means delivery targets get hit on a regular basis and change is now more predictable, the need for a safety net of added contingency at each layer will drop significantly.

In addition, the new collective approach to planning should ensure the leadership is more vigilant about what they sign up to and therefore more challenging about what's put in front of them. They will be conscious of avoiding the loss of valuable investments because capacity is unnecessarily tied up by inappropriate contingency – the opportunity cost of contingency can be significant. Consequently, contingency should be managed at the portfolio level and enable the following:

- Consistency across the portfolio in how it is calculated and applied.

- Aggregation of the contingency, and assurance it is put to the most effective and valuable use for the benefit of the investment as a whole.

- For it to be released once the need for it has passed and if appropriate, used to help areas struggling.

- Projects and programmes to be held to account for their use of contingency and prevent it becoming a series of personal stashes to bail out delivery problems not accounted for. As such this provides an incentive for tighter control over delivery.

- Control of the opportunity cost associated with the aggregated contingency.

- Assurance that every penny is spent wisely.

Contingency is not just money. It can be for any resource type, including time, and needs to be clear about exactly what it consists of, so that any deployment of it will work. For example, the monetary value given to contingency effort for internal staff is not the same as the cash value required to pay external bills to suppliers.

Balance the two in a rolling portfolio plan of 'now, next, later'

Having determined sufficient information about supply and demand, the next step is to balance the two in a plan that shows the optimum configuration of investments. What follows is based on getting a new plan together for the first time. Once this is done, the plan will be 'rolling'. As such, governing it will be about keeping it going with a constant check on balancing demand with supply in alignment with ambition. It is not about starting from scratch every year.

You will need a small planning group for this. This group should contain those familiar with the demand priorities and the supply constraints and at least one person who can create a good portfolio plan. You might not be surprised to learn I recommend using workshops.

To build the plan, use iterative modelling to find the best possible configuration that might not be readily visible. Some of the gaps in data and information will also not come to light until the modelling is underway. The plan should clarify the following for the organisation:

- What it is trying to achieve.
- Where it needs to invest.
- What it can safely cope with.
- How it can deliver value frequently.

It will also show the return on investment and therefore the extent to which change capability allows pursuit of ambition. The plan in the shape of a manageable workload is obviously key to turning failure into success. But producing such a plan can't be achieved by following the usual planning approach. That approach is amongst the practices that you have to be prepared to dispense with as part of the mindset pre-requisites. It is summarised below, followed by what will work in its place, which is based on the principles you have already been introduced to.

Planning practices to avoid – the 'Plan A' approach

The following is a description of what usually happens and why it is preventing a breakthrough. There will be variations on this theme, but the gist of it remains the same. I call this approach 'Plan A' because it has for some time been the default approach. What's needed is an alternative that will work to exploit air traffic control and the power of six…Plan B. Details of this are in the next section.

Plan A starts during the annual budgeting exercise, when the leadership team agrees some direction, high-level targets, and a 'budget' for change. Sometimes this is a clearly stated figure, sometimes it is only implied, by not having made a pronouncement, the current year figure is assumed to continue. Each department then goes off to agree its own change agenda. These separate agendas are brought together to see what they add up to. They usually have a familiar ring to them because of the cycle of failure. So, a lot of the contents of each list are already 'given'. There will be new ones on there as well, including next year's agenda and those that have been delayed to the point that they are now critical and must be done in the coming year. This will be particularly pertinent given the impact of COVID-19 and the delays causing the backlog to grow, so 2021 is at risk of being even more overburdened than usual.

Something like a central PMO function will have the thankless task of pulling together a consolidated list. And that is usually all it amounts to – a list of projects and programmes, not a coherent portfolio plan. It would be like air traffic control simply producing a list of all the flights the different airlines wanted to make without worrying too much about whether there's enough runway and air space to accommodate them all. As long as there are enough pilots and cabin crew and it is affordable then they're ready to go.

When the first iteration of the consolidated list is produced, it usually has the following features:

- It is way over the budget decreed for the coming year.

- Even without any analysis it is obviously far too much too do.

- A large number of initiatives 'roll over' from the current year into the next one. (Assuming the financial year is January to December, it means all the roll-overs are active on the 1st of January).

- Most if not all the new initiatives due to start in the next year have a default start of day one – January 1st, because they are so pressing.

- Building a picture of this and its demand for change resource (PMs, BAs, IT, Architects etc.) shows a 'ski-slope' (figure 5):
    - For a few months or so the level of demand is a great deal higher than the current change (PM, BA etc) resource levels, which themselves may be higher than what's budgeted for, because the new year has a budget reduction embedded.
    - The level starts to tail off as plans show initiatives 'finishing'.
    - By the time you reach July supply will outweigh demand noticeably and by September there'll be hardly any work at all. Of course, come January the following year there'll be loads to do again.

- Everyone knows the reality is that things will slip, so there will be some 'natural' smoothing. The slope will shift to the right. As such they are less exercised by the picture and ironically rely on failure to bail them out.

53

SKI SLOPE EFFECT OF UNMANAGED DEMAND - EXAMPLE

COURTESY OF PLAN A

*Full Time Equivalent

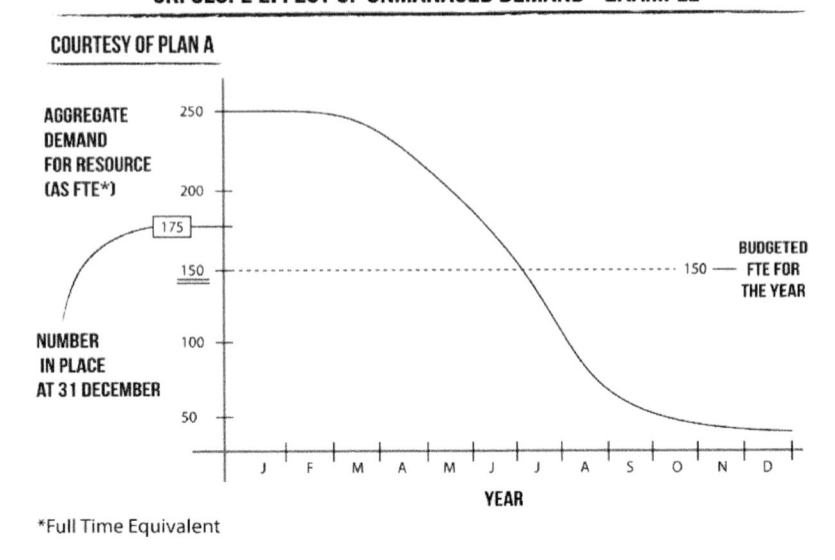

Figure 5: The Plan A ski-slope of demand

Other complications emerge to exacerbate the problem:

- If next year's change budget is different to this year's then there is a disconnect in funding for change staff between the 31st of December and the 1st of January. This opens up a lengthy exercise in how to make the current year and the next year 'connect' from day 1 or both of them will be compromised. It's a bit like an elevator stopping between two floors when the doors open. No-one's satisfied.

- If the expense rolling into day one in the new year is at odds with the budget, it means that counter adjustment is required in order to balance the books. So, if you start the year spending the equivalent of 50 FTEs more than budgeted for it means at some point you have to drop to at least 50 FTEs below budget for a similar length of time. Budget balancing then becomes the primary focus at the expense of the impact on delivery of the investments commissioned.

It is readily accepted that you can't hire and fire at the rate the plan suggests and that in any case, the delivery schedules for each of the initiatives contributing to this ski-slope are generally regarded as unreliable. Yet this situation still forms the starting point of discussion, because that's all there is and because so much is already committed.

However, because the primary concern is to get the list within budget, a period of 'bartering' takes place. Sometimes this goes on for months and often into the year they are supposed to be planning for. By which time the list has grown longer as people remember things left off at first and 'new' requirements have emerged in response to changes. And some deliveries are now forecasting a later delivery.

Eventually, a compromise is accepted, such as a projected 'overspend' on the basis that projects will fail to progress according to plan anyway, so the natural 'smoothing' will free up funds for projects that apparently had no budget at the outset. It may also include the postponement of projects that initially were critical but when put to the test turned out not to be. Or solutions turned out not to be the only option and a much more pragmatic alternative was settled upon. Because it's taken so long to get there no-one has the energy nor the courage to suggest it needs checking from a feasibility point of view because demand and supply may not balance.

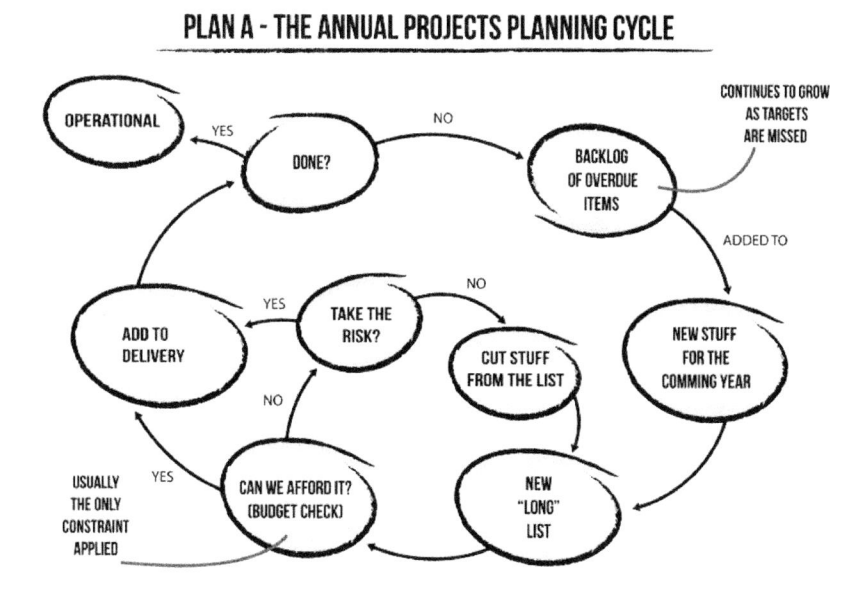

Figure 6: The Plan A project and programme annual planning cycle

Unfortunately, you are left with a plan that has been set up to fail. In the course of the year you will still spend close to what you thought you would overall, because you will have a work force in place that will cost the same, regardless of what it delivers. And many external commitments will have been incurred despite overall progress in delivery. But you won't get what you were expecting for it. The backlog has been added to as a result. Remember the cycle of failure?

The horse-trading has another negative connotation: it fosters a competitive rather than collaborative atmosphere amongst the leadership, which drags the change and IT teams into the mix. There's usually some alignment with change personnel to the business they support, so they start to get involved in strengthening the case for their business area. It also means business areas are likely to spend more than they or the organisation needs to at this early stage on analysis so that they come to the table more fully armed to help defend their corner.

It also lends itself to some non-collaborative practice like re-badging initiatives with a VIP status, such as 'regulatory', in order to get a pass onto the list at the expense of someone else's 'strategic' investment. There's no argument once it is a VIP. These initiatives get everything they want so they are largely immune to the effects of the demand / supply imbalance. Budget is much less of an issue, usually time and to some extent content are paramount. By getting what they need they are more likely to hit their targets.

Then there are the 'hidden' portfolios, mentioned earlier as symptoms of failing portfolio management – business areas commissioning work they don't notify others of until they have to – when for example, they need IT to install an application.

All of this entrenches the silo approach, when ideally you need the opposite. And it is an annual occurrence. So, every year the same cycle of budgeting and planning and contention takes place, with the same pattern and the same outcome. The cycle of failure.

Planning techniques to embrace – Plan B

The alternative to this purgatory is much more collaborative, a lot easier to get a coherent and achievable plan together and helps manage expectations about what can be done. And of course, it gets you the return you are looking for. It's the mindset pre-requisites in action. Above all, it is as close as you'll ever get to being able to guarantee delivery. And it brings together air traffic control and the power of six. Consequently, you get perpetual success in the shape of a continual stream of added value released.

PLAN B - THE CONTINUOUS PORTFOLIO PLANNING CYCLE

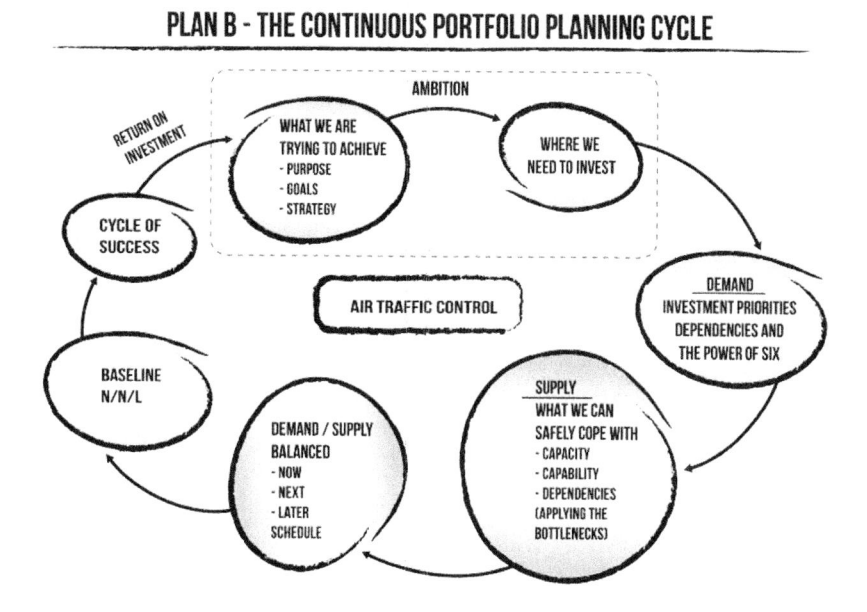

Figure 7: The Plan B portfolio planning cycle

Using the principle of the business process model, what you will need as inputs to this are the outputs from the previous Chapter:

- The ambition (what we are trying to achieve and where we need to invest).

- Information about the candidates for investment (from defining demand).

- The constraints (what we can safely cope with).

- The overall expected return on the investment – the gap to be bridged.

- And, hopefully it goes without saying by this time, the mindset pre-requisites.

The approach to accomplish all this is called 'zero-based planning', which is explained next.

Zero-based planning

There are three key principles to this that differ from the 'Plan A' approach:

1. The first is that it starts the plan with zero projects on it. No 'givens' or special cases, nothing. Hence the name. Anything to be considered, including those already up and running, needs to be argued on to the list, rather than amassing a large list of givens and potentials way beyond what can be coped with and then trying to argue off enough to make it manageable. It gives you your best chance of getting the right investment together with a manageable workload and not be constrained by attachments to previous commitments no longer of value. Like everything else, having done this once subsequent iterations will be a lot easier.

2. The second is that it makes sure that the plan is achievable before applying a final sense check on what the overall cost is. At first this might seem counter-intuitive, but you'll see that affordability (and risk) are taken care of automatically because the approach really does produce more from less. If cost and risk still prove unpalatable then adjustments can be made, but at least they can be done with confidence that the resulting plan can be delivered successfully.

3. The third is that the plan is 'rolling'. It is not annual. The portfolio plan is not like project and programme plans, it does not have a defined 'end'. In essence it is infinite. Like air traffic control, it continues while there are flights and journeys. It is subject to ongoing review and where necessary adjustment. You can of course place an annual view over the plan to see what is happening within each financial year, and formally review on a regular basis such as quarterly. Oversight is in any case continuous.

Prioritisation

Investment areas should already have been prioritised as part of the leadership deciding where it needs to concentrate its investment. As initiatives will have had to be argued onto the list by demonstrating how they contribute, they automatically come with an investment priority. This saves a lot of wasted time arguing the relative priority of individual initiatives competing with each other. If they pass the alignment test and are worthy of consideration, they will be considered in order of priority, but only be confirmed if they fit in.

As a result, you will end up with a 'now, next, later' sequence. Initially, this might seem like putting some things off that are regarded as urgent. Ironically, by virtue of putting them in a plan that will deliver, the start date might be deferred, but the end date is now much more assured than would have been the case when cramming it in and breaching constraints. In many respects, delivery is likely to be sooner as a result. So, in Plan B 'later' actually means 'sooner'.

Applying the supply side constraints and the power of six

The planning group should model the optimum configuration of investments balancing demand priorities with supply constraints – the bottlenecks. Obviously, demand should be applied in order of priority, though that priority might be compromised by the need to respect constraints. Whilst doing this the group should also look at what opportunities to exploit the power of six have already been identified in shaping the most important areas needing investment. It is uniquely placed to do this by having all the detail in front of them during the modelling and can spot where these opportunities are affected by the shape the portfolio is taking and where new opportunities emerge as a result. In balancing demand with the constraints, the group should make sure that:

- Any adjustments that can be made to increase throughput are considered.

- Their limits are respected.

- Any inputs to each of them are of the required quality so they can be readily processed.

- Lower priority tasks do not get in the way.

There will be some trial and error involved in this. Eventually, the group should find a plan that can be accommodated by the bottleneck(s), respects as far as possible the investment priorities, and has exploited the power of six. The aim is to get all the worthy investments scheduled on a 'now, next, later' basis, enabling the workload to be maintained at a manageable level and triggering the cycle of success.

It is possible that some of the initiatives will have to 'flex' their plans in order to accommodate each other when in contention at the bottlenecks. It is a case of finding whatever works to get to the point of being able to balance the plan, but without getting side-tracked into ongoing analysis (remember procrastination is the enemy). This is where 'small is beautiful' can provide some flexibility.

If you have a scheduling tool with 'what if' scenario planning to help you it will make this task much easier and quicker. If you don't have anything particularly sophisticated, you can still achieve the same aim but it might take a bit longer and you'll need to be a bit more pragmatic about the level of detail you go into to determine whether you have a problem. You will need to bear in mind the level of risk this might add to the portfolio and have some measures in place, particularly monitoring, in mitigation.

This may be a rash assumption, but it is that for those of you without a scheduling tool, you don't have a large, complex portfolio to deal with, otherwise you would have been compelled to install one by now. In that case you should be able to come up with something fairly simple based on the principles outlined so far. If this is not the case, then this exercise is telling you there's a dangerous gap in your capability.

Implications of the balanced delivery schedule – return on investment, risks and assumptions

During modelling, a portfolio schedule will begin to emerge, which the planning group should share with stakeholders to test acceptability for the following and provide an opportunity to make adjustments in the investments and their plans if necessary:

- The return on investment – is it good enough?
- The portfolio level risks – are they beyond an acceptable level?
- Assumptions underpinning the plan – what if they're wrong?

These need to be acceptable before confirming the optimum configuration and may help in deciding which configuration should be adopted. This is also the point at which it might become apparent that the ambitions are beyond what the organisation can cope with and those will have to be modified accordingly.

Implications of the balanced delivery schedule – affordability

Once you have a configuration that fits as best you can get it – the 'optimum' picture – you have reached the point that you know the extent to which you can safely invest. You are then able to check whether it is affordable. Because of the way the plan has been built, this should be a formality, but there are implications that might need to be addressed.

The organisation knows the risk of failure has been significantly reduced by the construct of the plan, so the stated overall cost and outcomes delivered by the investment are as reliable as they ever could be. Therefore, this test is about the appetite the organisation has for spending what now appears is required to deliver the optimum configuration of its priorities and any cost implications beyond that. This includes implications for the supply side utilisation. For example, the number of project managers or other 'change' staff required might now be much less than currently employed, so there may be redundancy costs. The 'now, next, later' schedule might also have implications for the arrangements with external suppliers. And, because the plan has been constructed on a rolling basis, rather than annual, it is also important to 'overlay' the financial years to understand how they are impacted and benefit from the configuration.

In terms of affordability, it comes broadly in two categories – external and internal expenditure. External expenditure is money out the door. Internal expenditure is the value placed on the use of the organisation's resources to get the work done. This is almost entirely human resource. Despite what monetary value might be attributed to this resource as a result of the financial model constructed for 'change', the core currency here is 'effort'. A few supplementary questions arise as a result of reaching the optimum configuration:

- Does it mean that some aspects of the supply side are significantly underutilised, because they are overstaffed compared to the capacity of the 'bottlenecks'?

- If so, is there any expense required to deal with this? It is a consequence of getting your house in order but must not be ignored.

Whether the 'cost' of the portfolio appears to be less or more than the organisation's appetite to spend, it has two options:

- To stick with it, knowing it can have confidence in the plan and the returns expected. Or
- Make adjustments.

The latter means going around the planning loop again to make sure that the resulting configuration of deliveries remains manageable. In the case of the cost appearing somewhat lower than there is money available, it is critical to remember that trying to spend more won't necessarily mean more gets done. In fact, by virtue of the balanced configuration you have come up with, trying to do more is taking you back to plan A and the cycle of failure. You are increasing the risk to everything in the portfolio. If you have some spending 'headroom' that you want to make use of then try applying it to some of the bottlenecks first in order to increase capacity for throughput.

Baseline the plan

The plan now has the safest, best value outcome possible with demand and supply balanced to maintain a manageable workload of 'now, next, later' investments. As such it replaces 'too much is top priority' in the cycle of failure and starts turning it into a cycle of success, as shown earlier. The baseline allows the impact of any potential variation to be readily assessed. You are now back in control of your future – the portfolio is working for you, not you for the portfolio.

Congratulations on getting this far. It is, however, only the starting point, albeit a hugely important one in gaining control of your future. What's needed next is a regime to sustain and build on what's been accomplished, keep the capability growing and the long-term investment safe, and success perpetuated. The measures needed to accomplish this are covered next.

Chapter summary

To turn the cycle of failure into a cycle of success you need to:

- Make the workload manageable, balancing demand with supply to enable a rolling plan of 'now, next, later' investments.

- Determine the organisational constraints that shape the capacity of supply by finding the bottlenecks and their limits – 'what can we safely cope with?'.

- Define demand by addressing 'what are we trying to achieve?' and 'where do we need to invest?' in order to succeed.

- Determine priority investment areas and look for synergies through the power of six.

- Appraise investment options on the basis of the extent they contribute to the ambition, how they fit alongside other investments when balancing with supply and to what extent they can be broken down into frequent value adding releases.

- Control contingency centrally.

- Use Plan B with a zero-based, iterative modelling approach to bring it all together.

- Assess the extent to which ambition can be achieved. Adjust if necessary.

- Sense check affordability and opportunities to invest in expanding capacity in bottlenecks.

- Baseline the plan.

5: How to keep the cycle of success turning faster

Use streamlined governance

A streamlined governance framework will make sure you retain a balanced portfolio, keep the workload manageable, hit targets and realise the best value outcomes continuously in line with ambition. It will also enable you to:

- Embed the new approach in 'the company way'.

- Promote the mindset pre-requisites, especially in acting as one, not silos.

- Oversee the growth in capability.

- Make sure spring cleaning is done all year round.

The framework needs to be a facilitator not an inhibitor. It must also stay 'streamlined'. Spring cleaning all year round will help enormously with this. It should include an authority that presides over the investment and its return, and an investment management facility to support the authority.

These two may sound similar to a portfolio steering committee and a central PMO. But as you will come to see in what follows, whilst it does cover much of the same ground, there are some important differences. To reflect them and to avoid any negative perceptions associated with the PMO 'brand' (such as 'admin centre') that unfortunately prevail in many organisations, you should call these two new entities something more in keeping with the impact they are intended to have.

I suggest Investment Authority (IA), rather than portfolio steering committee. The IA should be held to account for shaping, commissioning and delivering the investment in the future of the organisation and the realisation of the returns expected. To be clear, this is more than just steering the delivery of a collection of projects and programmes. It's about the ongoing end-to-end management of the investment in the future of the organisation.

The Investment Authority needs support that will look after the investment on a day-to-day basis and facilitate its successful outcome. You will see I refer to this body as the Investment Management Facility (IMF). The IMF should also, jointly with the IA, strive to grow capability.

To illustrate how these might fit in the governance framework, please see the example below. This is not an org chart, simply the collection of disciplines that need to support each other in pursuit of the organisation's ambition. Other than the IA and the IMF, the rest should already be in place in one way or another.

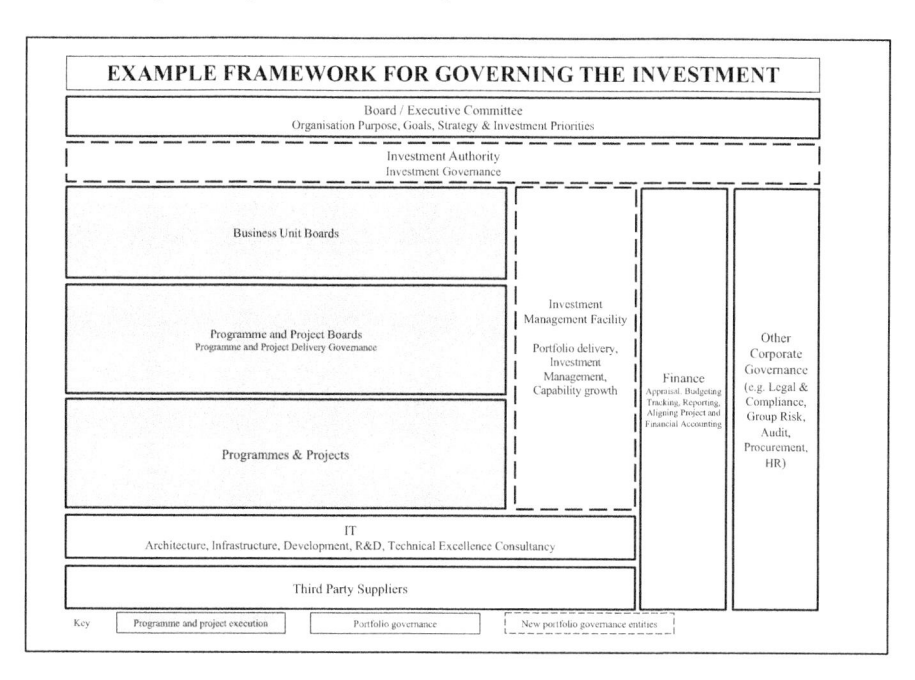

EXAMPLE FRAMEWORK FOR GOVERNING THE INVESTMENT

- Board / Executive Committee — Organisation Purpose, Goals, Strategy & Investment Priorities
- Investment Authority — Investment Governance
- Business Unit Boards
- Programme and Project Boards — Programme and Project Delivery Governance
- Investment Management Facility — Portfolio delivery, Investment Management, Capability growth
- Finance — Appraisal, Budgeting, Tracking, Reporting, Aligning Project and Financial Accounting
- Other Corporate Governance (e.g. Legal & Compliance, Group Risk, Audit, Procurement, HR)
- Programmes & Projects
- IT — Architecture, Infrastructure, Development, R&D, Technical Excellence Consultancy
- Third Party Suppliers

Key: Programme and project execution | Portfolio governance | New portfolio governance entities

Figure 8: Example high level governance framework

The principle roles played by each of these entities are illustrated in the example below.

Table 6: Principle roles in governance

Role	Responsibility
Board / Executive Committee	Organisation's purpose and goals, strategy, operational well-being,

	investment priorities, investment and risk appetite, and overall outcomes.
Investment Authority (IA)	Delegated authority from the board / exec to manage the investment portfolio within the parameters established above. To oversee the return on the investment and to sponsor the continued drive to improve capability.
Business Unit Boards	Shape and deliver their contributions to the corporate portfolio in collaboration with each other, the IA and the IMF. This includes project and programme delivery.
IT	Provision of the technical environment, technical expertise for the shaping and delivery of the portfolio, leading the investments in the technical estate.
Finance	Financial and management accounting, investment financials, expenditure, ROI, budgeting and accounting policy.
Other corporate governance bodies	Both as business units (see above) and as specialists with additional parameters to be considered in shaping and delivering the portfolio (see constraints).
Investment Management Facility (IMF)	Advice and support for the board and the IA to shape the investment, maintain the investment plan, oversee portfolio delivery (air traffic control and the power of six) and the return on the investment, own the governance framework, drive capability development.

What is described next is the basis for a 'target operating model' (TOM). The finer details will be different for each organisation, given every organisation to some extent is unique. What will also vary to some extent is the journey you take to get these things in place as a lot will depend on your starting point.

You should make as much use as you can of valuable assets you already have and enhance where necessary. There is obviously a risk associated with this in transporting inappropriate 'old' practices, customs and perceptions into the 'new', but this needs to be balanced with the need to avoid re-inventing the wheel. Spring cleaning can help in this respect. Consequently, the mindset pre-requisites are very important here, and will already have been cemented to some extent by adopting Plan B for the portfolio. The rebrand will also help.

Set up an Investment Authority (IA)

As long as the principles are followed and it has the required authority it doesn't matter if the IA is taken care of as part of the main management board or executive team meeting, or that a separate leadership team including executives is established to govern the investment. In any case, the IA must demonstrate the mindset pre-requisites. As a reminder they are:

1. Apply the principles of portfolio management, with air traffic control and the power of six.

2. Work together as one, not in silos.

3. Change is business as usual – the investment in the organisation's future and an integral part of its day-to-day operation.

4. Spring clean all year round.

5. Only people make things happen.

6. Small is beautiful – strive to get value released regularly.

7. Procrastination is the enemy of change.

In overseeing progress, the IA must concentrate on air traffic control and not the details of individual flights – these should be taken care of at the project and programme level. Example terms of reference are listed below – they are self-explanatory. The chair of the IA must have sufficient authority to discharge its responsibilities. It's more often than not a COO. In some cases, it has been the CEO and I've also seen a 'deputy' CEO and a CFO in this role. It doesn't really matter as along as the chair has delegated authority and the principles of a 'Cabinet' mentality prevails.

The number of attendees should be enough to make sure the decision-makers are included, but entourages and deputies without authority will risk procrastination, which as you know is the enemy of change. It should meet regularly, and the pattern determined by need, so be prepared for it to fluctuate.

Table 7: Example Terms of Reference for the IA

Attribute	Details
Membership	Chair: a CxO with appropriate authority over peers in this role. Members: Business unit executive members, CIO / Head of IT, Head of IMF. Others by invitation.
Objectives	To deliver the required return from the investment in alignment with ambitions. To achieve an ongoing balance of business priorities, operational constraints and the value of outcomes required. To keep the board (and wider stakeholder group) appraised of investment progress and recommend courses of action as required. To raise the level of organisational capability to become a source of competitive advantage.
Inputs	Management information on summary status, forecast and potential variations, capability requirements.

	Approvals and other decisions required.
	Direction from the board / exec, especially in relation to ambition.
	Other group governance committees' policies and tolerances affecting the investment.
Responsibilities	To shape the investment portfolio and the 'now, next, later' priorities.
	To keep the investment safe and aligned with purpose, goals and strategy.
	To approve business cases and investment expenditure.
	To approve changes and variations to the investment portfolio.
	To manage portfolio level contingency.
	To keep the organisation informed of progress with the investment.
Outputs	Investment and scheduling decisions.
	Agreement to release contingency and new funding.
	Reports on status and forecast.
	Recommendations to the board / exec and wider stakeholder group.
	Capability improvement strategy.

Build and activate an Investment Management Facility (IMF)

How to ensure the Target Operating Model is sound

There is a huge temptation to short-cut the design to a new organisation structure because everyone wants to know where they will fit in and what exciting new roles are on offer, or by contrast whether they will survive and feature in the new world at all. There are still too many 'restructures' based on nothing more than the publication by email of a new org chart. Unsurprisingly these new arrangements too often don't live up to expectations. As you will have gathered if you've got this far in the book, it is important to set things up to succeed.

The approach should ensure you design a target operating model that will work. This will also provide criteria for assessing progress towards implementation and enable a gap analysis to determine the extent to which you can leverage what you already have. You need to derive what it looks like from what it is charged with delivering and in what way. Designing it by addressing the points below in sequence will help accomplish this:

1. The purpose of the IMF.
2. The products and services the IMF is expected to deliver to fulfil its purpose.
3. The capabilities and competencies required to deliver the products and services.
4. How they must operate in a cohesive and dynamic mechanism.
5. The roles and responsibilities needed to discharge this.
6. The structure required to hold it all together.

Implementation can start once you are clear about what needs to be put in place. You don't have to wait for every last detail of the design to be completed. In some respects, the design is likely to be adjusted following live operational experience. There will be some trial and error involved, hence the need for iteration to be planned in. You will need a small team to help you with this and ideally it is the team that will operate the services, augmented by some expert help from external sources. Implementation strategy is covered later in this Chapter.

The purpose of the IMF

The purpose is principally three-fold:

- To support achievement of the organisation's ambitions through enabling effective investment management and the best possible value in return.

- To drive the organisation's capability to change to the level described in Chapter 1.

- To provide an enjoyable and rewarding environment in which to work.

By contrast it's useful to be clear about what it must not be:

- A policing authority.
- An admin 'centre'.
- A project and programme office – projects and programmes will still need these for support.
- 'Detached' from the main day-to-day business operations.
- Placed in a part of the hierarchy subordinate to those it is holding to account.

IMF products and services

The principles of service management work well in structuring the offering of products and services in a service catalogue. At the highest level are service lines. Beneath each service line are the service items that constitute the detail of what's provided and allow some means of measurement. The service items are where the products and artefacts (such as templates, reports, policies and framework processes etc.) are detailed. The operations of the IMF will obviously also need some artefacts to support it.

To illustrate the concept, an example of the sorts of service lines that will be relevant to the IMF, together with a brief explanation are in the table below:

Table 8: Example service lines for the IMF

Service Line	Description
Return on Investment (ROI) / Benefits realisation	Support for the leadership in shaping ambition, the investment required to achieve it, the implications of balancing demand with supply, the potential for exploiting synergies, and support for realisation of the return.
Governance	Shape and support a framework that facilitates successful investment planning and delivery, especially the NNL schedule. Alert and mobilise the right authorities to take effective action when needed. Together with the IA set governance policy for projects and programmes. Maintain overall control of the portfolio. Risk and issue management. Assumption testing. Dependency and contingency management. Ensure checks and balances are enough to facilitate success.
Portfolio planning and change control	Ensure all investments are aligned to the ambition of the organisation and balance priorities with constraints in a rolling portfolio plan. Apply the power of six, and opportunities to break deliveries into smaller, frequent value packages. Change control includes action to assess and accommodate any variations, balancing demand with supply. Own and maintain planning standards, such as those for estimating, use of contingency and the management of portfolio level risks, assumptions and dependencies.

Financial management	Portfolio financial management and analysis.

Investment decision support, business case appraisal, financial analysis, project accounting principles and an effective link with the corporate finance function to align the portfolio financials with the ledger. It is important that project accounting and financial accounting should be kept apart operationally. Financial accounting is for the corporate finance team, not for the portfolio, programme and project teams. Financial accounting is concerned with balancing the books. Project accounting is concerned with balancing supply and demand. |
| Assurance | Embed quality assurance into the process; facilitate health checks and reviews. There should be liaison with internal audit, group risk and other corporate governance functions. Management of any third-party engagement in health checks and remedies. |
| Management Information (MI) and Reporting, with data management | The single source of the truth.

Comprehensive management information to support timely intervention, decision making, overall control of the portfolio and continuous learning. Analysis and management of portfolio 'dashboards' and reporting for delivery performance, risks and issues.

It must be readily available, accurate, relevant and up to date. It should be succinct, simple to read, understandable and enable quality decisions and actions to be taken.

Ideally it is available digitally and in real time and allows 'self-service' for all, especially for |

	the leadership. It should include scenario modelling.

The integrity of the data on which it is based is critical as is the effectiveness and security of the mechanism for sourcing and collating it. A good PPM system installed well, will help enormously with this.

Stakeholder communication in general falls under this – it isn't just about producing reports. |
| Delivery Support | This is about active engagement in major initiatives as part of risk mitigation and delivery assurance. In other words, having direct involvement to help keep things on track by taking relevant aspects of the service provision directly into the running of the initiative.

This also includes support for project and programme management offices – PMOs – to help them support the initiatives they are dedicated to. |
| Resource management | Provision of a complete resource picture, balancing supply and demand. A comprehensive forward look of demand with a relevant ambition-led time-horizon of, for example, 18-24 months.

Scenario modelling and predictive analysis.

Skills and capability gap analysis. Augmentation of supply on a planned and controlled basis. |

	Proactive in keeping demand in a manageable state and must work closely with all resource owners to control the supply side.

Co-ordination of investment to improve bandwidth in bottlenecks and the sourcing strategy should be agreed with resource owners.

Close liaison with resource owners to support ongoing development in capability. |
| Learning and capability development | Spearheading growth in change capability to a level of advantage. Training, coaching, mentoring, internal consultancy and any general advice on the whole nature of change, the investment portfolio and the growth in capability. These services should be delivered across the organisation, they are not just for change teams. This should be ongoing and informed by teams' and individuals' development plans and organisational learning loops and supported by liaison with external agencies and other sources of information and learning that could assist growth in capability.

This is also the vehicle for enabling transition into the IMF for career progression and capability growth to mutually benefit from the experience. |
| Asset custody | Master copies of artefacts.

This is sometimes known as the configuration library. It's the official record of the major artefacts associated with the ongoing investment portfolio. These include master copies of key documentation, such as baseline plans, investment priorities, business cases, |

	governance and other records that must be kept for auditing purposes and the learning process.
Methods, tools and process	To select, deploy and administer an effective suite of tools to support the shaping, control and delivery of the portfolio. It should include standards, methods and workflow. It does not include the technical tools and methods used by IT for software development but has an input to enable informed decision-making. It should enable the co-existence of multiple methods environments and the pragmatic use of best practice principles. Where necessary it should engage with third parties.

Capabilities and competencies required

To provide the products and services summarised above, the IMF will need the following capabilities. They are in no particular order:
- Strategy development and investment alignment.
- Organisational change leadership.
- Portfolio planning and change control.
- Portfolio governance.
- Stakeholder and relationship management at all levels.
- Data analysis and MI production.
- Demand and supply / resource management.
- Resource management.
- Financial management, investment management and economic appraisal.
- Risk and issue management.
- Business process engineering.
- Analysis and problem solving.
- Procurement and effective selection and use of methods and tools.
- Team leadership.
- Team working and collaboration.
- People management and development, coaching and mentoring.

Overall, the IMF should strive to become a highly respected and highly valued integral part of the organisation. There may well remain a perception amongst others that the IMF is the PMO 'of old'. It's remit, service catalogue, position in the organisation as well as the new brand will go some considerable way towards correcting this. However, there will be personnel in the IMF that were previously in the PMO and it is important that these are equipped and supported to be able to operate at the new level as quickly as possible. These need to be repositioned as much as the PMO itself becoming an IMF.

The following competencies will be needed to underpin the capabilities. To clarify, the difference between the capabilities and the competencies in this context is broadly that the capabilities will enable successful discharge of responsibilities and achievement of goals, whereas the competencies are the attributes that will enable the capabilities to be effective. You'll see the subtle difference between them in the detail listed.

As an example, without commercial acumen the capability to plan might be missing an opportunistic dimension or a sense of pragmatism – it's not enough just to be excellent at putting a plan together – it's also about recognising what the plan is attempting to achieve. As with the above, these are examples to get you started, not a prescription.

Table 9: Example competencies for the IMF

Competency type	Attributes
Commercial Acumen	Customer focussed. Strategic mind-set, investment, outcome and ROI focussed. Commercially astute. Financial awareness / project accounting. Pragmatic. Minimalist in processing for maximum value outcome.
Leadership	Inspirational. Motivating. Resource management and people development. Confidence.

	Imaginative. Innovative and a catalyst by nature. Rapid learning and continuous improvement. Anticipate and act fast. Facilitate success not prevent failure. Make things happen. Lean operations. Streamlined team organisation operation – agile by nature.
Technical	Portfolio management. Programme and project management. Multi-method environments. Planning and estimating. Technical tools expertise, for example, portfolio management tools, often referred to as PPM. Risk management.
Engagement	Stakeholder management and relationship building. Effective communication, listening, understanding, being understood and influencing. Feedback facilitation. Team players, collaborative and mutually supportive.
Analysis	Business operations and data analysis. Problem solving. Scenario analysis.

Operations and Workflow

Your TOM will need to show, even if at a high level only, how the IMF will operate, particularly in its interaction with other functions, inside and outside of the organisation. The detail of this will vary in each organisation and need to be worked through to make sure data and workflow are connected with the constituent parts of the framework (see figure 8).

I use a variety of tools to help with this, including Porter's Value Chain (Michael E. Porter, (1985)), flow charts, systems maps, and 'swim lanes' diagrams. These can be particularly powerful in supporting the communication plan during and after implementation of the IMF.

Roles, Responsibilities and Structure – the 'pooling' effect

The roles should be constructed bearing in mind that their purpose is to facilitate success by enabling the best possible outcomes. They should also provide for a thoroughly rewarding working environment. This requires embedding flexibility, mutual learning and support, development, enabling wider service coverage and avoiding knowledge and skill dependency. This is achieved with a pool of people working across all areas, rather than putting individuals in scoped roles that operate in silos. Each member should lead on one or two service lines and provide support on one or two others. There should be some form of rotation to keep growth in learning and strengthening capability, and workload should be kept manageable. Obviously. The arrangements should be balanced with the career aspirations and development needs of the members. There's no need for a formal hierarchy save for the nominated leader of the IMF, though there will be obvious differences in expertise and experience, which should be recognised and shared for mutual benefit.

This arrangement fosters a sense of community. Every team member should feel that they have the backing of everyone else on the team. Whatever they are engaged in, especially if it's supporting a major programme, they must not feel isolated. If one fails, they all fail – if they all support each other, everyone succeeds. There is a wealth of experience at their disposal, so it makes sense to use it for mutual benefit. The team works more cohesively on this basis and is more effective at adding value, sharing knowledge and growing capability faster. It also acts as an effective communication, knowledge and learning conduit for the whole organisation, not just the change community. The role of the leader is critical in facilitating this. I've used this 'community' style approach many times and it makes a real difference to the people involved, their performance and the level of value added. There's an example of this in the section on training and development, further on in this Chapter.

In allocating lead and support roles for each service line you need to know broadly how much effort will be required to discharge the responsibilities. Use 'Full Time Equivalent' (FTE) rather than number of heads for this. It will allow greater flexibility in deploying resource and more readily enable flexible working. Aggregate the total effort and then decide how to apportion it across the services provided. You may require greater emphasis in one area versus another, albeit for a limited period, as the emphasis is likely to change according to circumstances. The point about this model is to keep it fluid so the allocation can fluctuate.

The pooling effect does not sit comfortably with traditional organisation structures because of their inherent hierarchies and job silos. So, to help you get started, a simple example of the community approach is below, showing current leads and support for each service line. This approach might take a bit of time to get used to, especially if the environment is very hierarchical and grade conscious. In that sense the IMF will feel it is pioneering. However, I guarantee, based on experience, that once a pioneer starts making some headway a lot faster than the others, the rest will follow.

Service Line	Current Lead (name)	Current Support (name(s))
Return on Investment (ROI) / Benefits realisation		
Governance		
Portfolio planning and change control		
Financial management		
Assurance		

Management Information (MI) and Reporting, with data management		
Delivery Support		
Resource management		
Learning and capability development		
Asset custody		
Methods, tools and process		

Figure 9: Example IMF structure to illustrate the 'pooling effect'

To help manage deployment, learning and development planning, mutual support and therefore bringing the team together, I recommend using a simple support and development matrix – there is an example below. The skills and experience don't have to be restricted to the service lines of the IMF. If there are others that the team and its members would mutually benefit from then there is no reason not to share these too. At some point it might be possible to extend this to those not in the IMF but are either on their way in or are looking for help in developing their capability in change. This is another means by which capability growth and embedding the approach in the 'company way' can both be progressed.

Team member	Major skill / experience to help others with	Skill / experience to get help from others
Ian Other	Portfolio planning	Financial management
Simone One-else	MI and reporting	Portfolio planning
Anne D'Another	Financial management	MI and reporting

Figure 10: Example, mutual support and development matrix; input to service leads / support roles

Team Leadership attributes

Selecting the right leader for this role is critical. The capabilities and competencies have already been summarised above. The leader must be someone completely in tune with the ambitions, the sentiments and the mindset pre-requisites of the new approach. This is especially true of the need to lead a team outside of the conventional hierarchical and silo approach and in an environment when it is increasingly likely that, post-COVID, remote and flexible working might well be the default, rather than the exception. The leader must have the gravitas to take this forward with the organisation's leadership team, and the organisation as a whole, particularly those with influence. What's needed is a charismatic and inspirational leader who recognises the need to operate as a figurehead and as a servant and who will strive to take the organisation towards the vision described in Chapter 1.

Where should it sit?

Operationally, the IMF will report to the IA. From an organisational point of view, it is imperative that its operational position is not compromised and as such ideally it should report into the CxO that will chair the IA. It needs to work with the change practitioners and the lines of business as an independent 'critical friend', there to support the safe shaping and delivery of the investment. It must be able to challenge unhindered when necessary for the good of the organisation's future. There's no room here for cultural pecking orders or grading considerations. If you don't put the IA in an authoritative position, it won't have the impact needed. Would you subordinate air traffic control to one of the airline's managers? All the wonderful progress made up to this point could be completely negated if this facility is 'neutralised' because of where it is positioned.

Implementation strategy

Implementation of the IMF should not be a 'big bang'. It should follow the principle of small is beautiful and be in phased releases that build on each other, exploit the power of six, and release value regularly. The plan should balance this with logical dependencies and the capacity to build and implement. How the plan should look in detail will depend on your circumstances, but there is a high-level example in this section to help you get started. The plan will also need to accommodate a transitional period during which the 'current' arrangements are phased out alongside adoption of the 'new' ones.

It's also useful to follow some implementation principles for delivery assurance and to keep the operation running during transition. Some suggestions are below:

- The operational IMF team must be capable of receiving and effectively operating the new products and services as they are implemented.

- A 'design authority' should be employed to check what's built is in line with what's needed, and everything remains joined up.

- Likewise, builders of processes and artefacts must develop them jointly and conduct peer reviews.

- Products should be 'showcased' with the team and include a proposal for stakeholder engagement and an implementation strategy. The purpose of the showcase is to agree that the product is in line with ambition, fits with other products and can be shared with the wider stakeholder group prior to implementation. It also helps in applying the power of six.

- The wider community should be engaged in this transition as much as is practicable. This will help understanding and a feeling of some ownership in what emerges.

- A communication strategy and a plan for its execution to underpin the implementation is imperative. Communication must start early and be regular, consistent, simple, engaging and informative throughout and beyond implementation. Ideally you should get support from marketing and communications experts inside and outside of the organisation and make sure you engage them at the outset, well before even some of the planning has begun.

Table 10: Example of a high-level IMF phased implementation plan

Phase	Products and Services
1	High level governance framework. Communications and Stakeholder Engagement. Operational arrangements.
2	Resource Management. Delivery Assurance. Portfolio Governance and Planning Frameworks and Processes. Financial Management Framework. Benefits Management Framework. MI and Reporting.
3	Risk Management. Configuration Management. Contingency Management. Best practice standards, methods, tools and processes. Learning & Development Framework. KPIs / measures.

Embed the approach in 'the company way'

The new approach and the principles that underpin it need to become part of the organisation's paradigm, particularly its culture. They should be adopted in policies, values, training and educational material. They should appear in 'onboarding' new staff (whatever terms they are engaged on, so yes that means contractors too) so that all the usual channels and messages, formal or informal that are used to convey 'how we work' contain the right messages and support for following them.

It is critical that the organisation's performance management system is aligned with the new approach to encourage and reward the right behaviour. If everything else is in place but people are rewarded for following the old approach and penalised for following the new one, then you've wasted your time. In this sense, performance management includes the formal, usually annual, appraisal system that influences career prospects and remuneration, and the informal judgements throughout the year that signal to people what will be received favourably and vice versa. Obviously, there is a balance to be struck between remaining open-minded to continue to learn and improve, whilst remaining vigilant to the danger of the return of the sentiments that drive the cycle of failure. As the new arrangements become embedded in the company way, it will become a lot easier to tackle this.

Retraining autopilot

Critical to embedding the new arrangements in the company way is retraining 'autopilot'. As change is only ever given effect by people, and people are motivated to think and act in one way or another by a number of factors, it stands to reason that if you nurture the people in the right way they will do the rest for you. The internal mechanism that makes people think and act in the way they do, especially in times of stress and when under pressure is like autopilot. In other words, it's the survival instinct that comes to the rescue when they have no time to think. In a corporate setting autopilot's conditioning is developed over years. If autopilot has been developed to think of change as a list of mostly discretionary projects and programmes, delivered via a series of silos, then it will struggle to operate with the new approach when put under pressure. Chapter 3 introduced the mindset pre-requisites for adopting the new approach that would lead to the cycle of success. Autopilot needs retraining to adopt those pre-requisites.

The leadership team and those involved in supporting them will have had some practical experience applying pre-requisites to get the new baseline portfolio plan in place, particularly working together rather than in silos. As a result, it will be a lot easier for the rest of the organisation to follow that example. But that won't be enough. Training, development, coaching, further practical experience and a supportive environment will be needed too. The desired impact of this retraining won't happen overnight, but immersion in an environment that supports the new mindset and the practices that go with it, will make it happen a lot quicker.

Think of retraining autopilot in terms of learning a new language. You won't become fluent after a few hours in evening classes learning the basic structure of the language, some everyday phrases and a few verb conjugations, especially when the classes are the only place you speak it. Even in the classes, you will revert to your first language to cope with a difficult situation. To become fluent, and quickly, you need to immerse yourself in the language and its culture, to live in an environment where you have to use the language to survive.

It is the same with the mindset pre-requisites and the new approach. The organisation needs to be immersed in them for them to take hold as the default and become part of the new autopilot. The leadership, the IA and the IMF all have a part to play in making this happen. Steps required to do this are covered next.

Continue to grow capability

Training and development

The mindset pre-requisites reinforce the need to continue to develop and motivate people – without them change won't happen, without developing and nurturing talent capability won't grow. When it does it perpetuates success. Therefore, the IMF should provide or facilitate the provision of appropriate training and development on an ongoing basis. This includes coaching and mentoring, supported learning on the job as well as training events and engagement of external agencies to share learning and experience. The training should be aimed at project, programme and portfolio levels and at the entire organisation, not just change delivery teams. It is vital that the capability to deliver projects and programmes is good enough to support the portfolio and as part of the drive to get change into the organisation's DNA it must include everyone.

Training events should be relevant, timely, lead to practical application during or immediately following the event and tailored to suit the learning style preferences of those attending. You will need to ensure that any such events and those providing them, particularly externals, are aligned with the mindset pre-requisites and the new approach. These events must provide deeper understanding of portfolio management, aid the retraining of autopilot and make a noticeable difference in capability. In that respect, things to be wary of are:

- Classroom based only (virtual or physical), not practical application in the field, and focussed more on passing a memory test to get a certificate rather than embedding knowledge, skills and understanding.

- An absence of portfolio principles (even as context) such as air traffic control, the power of six and balancing demand with supply.

- Reinforcing the 'change' versus 'business as usual' perspective.

- Lacking an entrepreneurial view of change as an investment in the future of the organisation and how it holds together purpose, goals, strategy and operations.

- Overstressing the significance of methods, tools, frameworks and processes at the expense of good business management, common sense and collaboration of people working towards a common goal.

As part of its facilitation of learning and development across the change community and beyond, the IMF should look for opportunities to employ those who want to move into change, try a different perspective in change or gain insight and experience of change on their way to leadership. By giving tomorrow's leaders an early taste of how to manage organisational change as an investment delivered in a portfolio, they will be much better equipped when exercising responsibility for selecting and directing investment in the future.

The IMF should also use a range of promotional opportunities at leadership meetings and staff events to share the message, answer questions, showcase progress in capability growth and share experiences. Holding a regular series of 'fitness' sessions with a range of staff from all areas around the organisation in small groups to exchange news, views and feedback, generate ideas and keep in touch with the 'shop floor' should also feature. Addressing three high level questions can provide a bit of a framework for this and has shown to be highly effective in fostering collaboration and a community spirit:

- How can we continue to improve our service to our stakeholders (internal and external to the organisation)?
- How can we work together to develop as a community?
- How can we support each other in developing ourselves as individuals?

I have used this approach before, and it is striking how effective it is, noticeably with one group of over 60 project and programme managers, many of whom hadn't previously met, had a wide variety of professional backgrounds, were serving different parts of the organisation and were based in different locations. They'd all just come through a rather bruising restructuring and downsizing exercise. Bringing them together in a 'community launch day', posing the three questions above and facilitating action in coming up with answers and an action plan was all it needed to get it started. The introduction to that day made clear how strong they were as a group and how their future was solely in their hands – no-one was going to do this for them. This group had between them well over 500 years' experience in delivering change. Pointing that out and the fact that it would cost millions in any currency to buy in that level of experience from external agencies and even that would be lacking 'inside' knowledge, made it clear how important, how strong and therefore how valuable to the organisation they were as individuals and more so as a coherent group – that so much more strength came from harnessing their experience as a community than working as a collection of 60 individuals operating in silos. It would feel like all 60 of them were working on every project or programme – no-one would feel isolated, the whole team was behind each of them, continuously. It gave the group a tremendous boost in confidence and led to a remarkable uplift in performance.

Activate a learning loop

In addition to the fitness sessions and promotional opportunities, the IMF must facilitate and drive continuous learning to keep the organisation ahead of the game. Lessons learned reports help to some extent but a lot more is needed. Often, they're produced well after the event and don't have an effective vehicle for implementing what's been learned. By contrast the learning loop must operate continuously. In terms of capturing the information 'real time' from current delivery activities, sources include, but are not limited to, risk mitigation outcomes, issues and their resolutions, minutes of governance meetings, health checks and project, programme and portfolio reviews and audits. You can easily capture lessons learned along the way by including them as part of the Risk, Assumptions, Issues and Decisions (RAID) log, so RAID becomes RAIDL.

The fitness sessions and promotional activities should also be used to elicit feedback that will help. In general, there should be an 'open door' to the IMF on an ongoing basis for people to share ideas for improvement. It benefits everyone. As you will have seen from the operating model proposed for the IMF, the fluidity of the IMF resource enables mutual learning on a faster and greater scale than if they operated in silos.

The IMF will need to ensure it records the learning and feeds it through the channels it uses to guide and support delivery across the portfolio at project and programme level as appropriate. This might include policies and frameworks, coaching, mentoring, training and development as well as the construction and ongoing oversight of the portfolio plan, and management of risks, and of course through the fitness sessions and promotional exercises referred to above.

Keep it fit and healthy

Legacy practices

Despite the best efforts to get everything in place, there will undoubtedly be some legacy practices from the organisation's environment that could inadvertently cause problems for the new arrangements. Applying the principle of 'spring clean all year round' can help get rid of these.

Of those that are directly related to change, there are some obvious candidates. These are the checks and balances put in place as safety nets for projects and programmes to prevent failure. Because the rate of failure will have plummeted once the underlying cause has been addressed, the need for these safety nets will disappear. This will certainly save considerable time and cost. Addressing this is next.

Project and programme failure remedies – which ones to keep, which to ditch

There will always be room for improvement in project and programme delivery. The question is, which of the remedies currently applied will flourish and add real value once the underlying cause of failure has been addressed, and which must be dispensed with or they will drain resource, stifle progress and destroy value?

The reasons cited for project and programme failure are widely documented and usually boil down to deficiencies in leadership, organisation (including methods and processes), skills, communication and control. These have rightly been identified as areas where improvement will pay dividends. The remedial action is usually aimed at competency, operations (including methods, processes, tools and systems) and organisation (the operating model, structure, roles and responsibilities). The remedies can be distinguished in two other important aspects, which I refer to as Type A and Type B:

- Type A remedies are designed to facilitate success.
- Type B remedies are designed to prevent failure.

Although the definitions might seem pedantic, they are important, because from this you can identify which ones have the potential to add value – Type A, and which must be dispensed with – Type B. Type A remedies are investments in capability. They include competencies and aspects of operation and organisation that will raise the level of performance for the longer term, enhancing speed and accuracy. Examples are appropriate training and development and streamlined governance. Type B remedies are usually compensating measures – additional arrangements put in place because Type A remedies don't appear to have had the fully desired effect. They are much more likely to feature as operational or organisational remedies, such as new checks and balances, new committees and sign-off requirements or when the impact of a restructure such as centralising or decentralising the change function, turns out to be not much more than some people getting a new boss. Sometimes they appear as competency-related remedies, such as blanket training, regardless of skills and timing needs. The presence and proliferation of Type B remedies are a good indication that the underlying cause of delivery failure remains unaddressed.

Once the underlying cause is addressed, Type A remedies will fulfil their potential and add significantly more value. By contrast, Type B remedies will slow things down and drain your resource. They are also likely to become bottlenecks and so wrongly tempt you to reduce your throughput unnecessarily if you leave them in place.

Many of your Type B remedies are likely to be obvious, but it's worth applying some tests to weed out the more obscure. The sample list of questions below should help you in this respect. This list is not exhaustive, it is to prompt thinking as much as to provide direction – some may help more than others – so if you think of any that might help even more then please use them. You may even want to try a 'zero-based' approach to this, start with nothing and then argue remedies into place if they pass the right tests, rather than the other way around.

Area	Test
General	Is it geared more towards facilitating success, or is it trying to prevent failure? If it were removed, would delivery risk increase significantly? If it were removed, would delivery speed up and / or cost less without compromising quality and benefit value? Can it be justified on a cost / benefit basis or does the cost and time of its presence outweigh the value of what it is trying to protect?
Meetings	How many governance committees, and working parties are there, what are they for,

	how frequent are they and how many of them are attended by broadly the same group of people?
Checkpoints	How many checkpoints are there, whether formal or informal, that require approval before proceeding, and if missed would not compromise delivery, but speed it up?
Reporting	How much information, volume and detail, is required to be submitted before approvals can be considered? How many different variations of the same reports are being produced each week and month, and for what? How lengthy and detailed are the reports? Are they way beyond what is required for informed decision-making? How 'old' is the information in the reports by the time it gets to the decision-makers? Which checks and balances require additional occurrences of management information (MI) that have already been previously submitted to those concerned?
Sign-off	Amongst those 'signing-off', which of them has no accountability for, responsibility for or dependence upon what they are giving their approval for?
Testing	In application development, is the end-to-end testing (systems testing through to the final acceptance tests) disproportionately higher than the rest of the undertaking.

Table 11: Example tests to identify Type B remedies

All Type B remedies create a requirement for additional resource and management time. In some cases, this is considerable. And of course, if you employ additional people focussed on preventing failure, they will generate additional work to demonstrate their worth, involve others (for mutual support, or as a natural defence in case anything gets questioned) and require more time of those actually trying to get change delivered. Before you know it, you have an empire. Because it grows by stealth, it's hard to spot before it's become too large to deal with. The overhead on this is enormous.

Eliminating Type B remedies will therefore release value and enable the cycle of success to increase in speed. The longer they are left in place, the longer it will be before you get the portfolio fully working for you.

A comment on PPM tools

Portfolio, programme and project management (PPM) tools can be very effective in helping you establish and run a balanced rolling portfolio of investments, but it is critical that you establish need and practicality first rather than just buy whatever looks good. By virtue of having been through what is required to produce and govern a portfolio plan and governance framework, you should be much better placed to shape a requirement and test any tool for its suitability to support you in this endeavour.

To get the best from whatever you use, you must ensure any tool is implemented effectively and that data integrity is preserved. There's a long-standing joke that the worst implementations are those delivered by change teams to change teams. Bizarre though it might sound, I've seen many examples of poor procurement, implementation and usage of these tools. And poor implementations of these tools are merciless in their impact on cost and operation, so much so it would have been better without them. By contrast, I've witnessed good ones. And when they are good, they are very, very good. So, select and implement carefully, and then make sure you make full use of them. And remember, just like change in general, the tool is there to work for you, not the other way around.

In terms of recommendations to help you get started, there is plenty of research material publicly available. Amongst it you will find Gartner reviews and its 'magic quadrant', which is worth looking at. From first-hand experience I can say that in general, PPM tools are far more user-friendly and fit-for-purpose compared to say ten years ago. They much more readily acknowledge the portfolio level challenges covered in this book. I've used several of them over the years, including Clarity, HP PPM, MS Project Server and most recently Planview (Enterprise One), which I found easy to use and effective in supporting the sorts of activity described above.

In terms of ownership, the IMF should drive the selection, implementation, usage and ongoing assessment of portfolio management tools, and support the selection of tools and methods underpinning programme and project delivery. As you would expect, the emphasis as always should be on facilitating success, improving the chances of a high quality and faster outcome, rather than trying to avoid failure. The right tools implemented in the right way will make it much easier to keep change working for you.

Chapter summary

To build on the new arrangements and continue to grow capability, thus keeping change forever working for you, the following is needed:

- A streamlined portfolio governance framework.

- An Investment Authority to govern, on behalf of the board, the investment in the future of the organisation, as well as the delivery of the portfolio of projects and programmes and to sponsor the growth in capability. It's more than a portfolio steering group.

- An Investment Management Facility to support the IA by facilitating the investment, overseeing delivery of the portfolio and leading growth in capability. It's more than an Enterprise PMO.

- A pooling effect to deploy the skills and experience in the IMF.

- Implementation of the IMF in value-adding steps not 'big bang'.

- Embedding the new arrangements in the 'company way'.

- Retraining autopilot.

- Training and development, communication, 'fitness sessions' and wider engagement to help grow learning and capability.

- Ditching legacy initiatives and practices, Type B remedies, that no longer add, but destroy value.

- Select and use PPM tools with care – make them an accelerator, not a brake on realising return on the investment and continued growth in capability.

Summary

There's never been a more critical time to get change working for you. It will be the difference between long-term success, being an also-ran and failing. For too long, organisations have trapped themselves in a cycle of failure and suffered its consequences of high cost, low value return and thwarted ambition. And despite extensive efforts to escape in all that time, they remain stuck there. And that's because they haven't been using the right escape route. They need a plan B and this book provides it, together with a key to break free and a map to follow the road to success, by helping you address the following:

1. What you are trying to achieve.
2. Where you need to invest.
3. What you can safely cope with.
4. How you maintain the balance between them in a manageable workload of NNL investments.
5. How air traffic control and the power of six will get you higher returns, safer and faster.
6. How to continue to get better at all the above.

There's no reason for any organisation anywhere that runs projects and programmes to remain trapped any longer. And if you're still wondering whether you truly are incarcerated then ask yourselves this:

- Is your project and programme failure rate more than 10%?

- Does your portfolio look much the same year after year?

- Are the C-suite often frustrated that they are not able to rely on change to deliver expected outcomes?

- Do parts of your organisation continue to run 'hidden' portfolios of change?

- Are some areas trying to grow their own capability or circumnavigate the governance processes?

- Do you have a proliferation of Type B remedies trying to prevent failure?

- Do you build your portfolio in silos?

- Do you centralise, decentralise then recentralise your change function regularly?

- Do you wish you could wave all this away, replace it with perpetual success and be like the organisation described in Chapter 1?

Well, you have what you need, so set yourselves free, once and for all!

And finally

I do hope you have enjoyed this book and that it has demonstrated how relatively easy it is to get change working for you, compared to a highly expensive and lengthy transformation programme that comes up with a variation on the current arrangements and as such leaves you trapped.

Once you do get change working for you, you will enjoy perpetual success. It does require a shift in mindset, and I know from experience they don't come easily, hence the Chapter on mindset pre-requisites, which is designed to help you get the shift you need more readily. There's a very big prize on offer and you don't need to bet your life on trying to grab it. If anything, it's far riskier not to try. As I said at the outset – every organisation can do this, including yours. The sooner you start, the sooner you'll have change working for you, and the sooner you'll reap the rewards.

I sincerely wish you every success!

John
29 September 2020

Acknowledgements

I owe a debt of gratitude to all those I've worked with over the years that have helped deliver change, shape my experience and learning and thus enabled this book to be written. I especially thank those who have played a very important part in helping me get it into shape by offering so much of their valuable time, expertise and sound advice to make sure I got the message right, and in the right way: Jacob Abboud, Claire Gettinby and Peter Shirley especially in that respect. Others whose advice has also been invaluable, include Mark Buchan, whose book on agile transformation *Leaders it's not how you finish it's how you start,* is a must read for anyone involved in agile transformations.

Roberta Kapsalis turned my sketchy pencil drawings into excellent representations of informal diagrams, exactly as I needed. If you're ever in need of help with graphics, then I highly recommend her. She can be reached on 'Greek Goes Keto' robertakapsalis@gmail.com. And Michelle Davadoss, who's patience and marketing expertise helped me develop the way some of my advice is represented.

There are many more, and I apologise for not mentioning them all individually, but the final word must go to my dear long-suffering partner Gillian Waterworth, who could probably cite every word from every draft, and has spent the last ten months having to deal with the emotional roller-coaster this aspiring writer has been through, desperate to tell his story in an engaging, compelling, enjoyable and easy to apply way, and working at whatever time of day or night inspiration decided to make an appearance. I couldn't have asked for a more patient, understanding and loyal supporter.

Index of Illustrations and tables

Illustrations

Figure 1: The cycle of failure
Figure 2: The cycle of success
Figure 3: Where do we need to invest?
Figure 4: Change is the glue keeping ambitions and investment in line
Figure 5: The Plan A ski-slope of demand
Figure 6: The Plan A project and programme annual planning cycle
Figure 7: The Plan B portfolio planning cycle
Figure 8: Example high level governance framework
Figure 9: Example IMF structure to illustrate the 'pooling effect'
Figure 10: Example mutual support and development matrix

Tables

Table 1: Bottleneck attributes
Table 2: Bottleneck examples
Table 3: Example, 'what are we trying to achieve?'
Table 4: Example management tools for 'where do we need to invest?'
Table 5: Example, 'where do we need to invest?'
Table 6: Principle roles in governance
Table 7: Example Terms of Reference for the IA
Table 8: Example service lines for the IMF
Table 9: Example competencies for the IMF
Table 10: Example of a high-level phased IMF implementation plan
Table 11: Example tests to identify Type B remedies

References

Boston Consulting Group (BCG) (2020), Winning the '20s: https://www.bcg.com/featured-insights/winning-the-20s/science-of-change

Buchan, Mark (2019). Leaders it's not how you finish it's how you start, *The Agile Leader Ltd.*

Cox, James F., Schleier, John G. (2010). Theory of Constraints Handbook, *McGraw-Hill Education.* ISBN 9780071665544.

Cox, Jeff; Goldratt, Eliyahu M. (1984). The goal: a process of ongoing improvement. *Great Barrington, Massachusetts: North River Press.* ISBN 0-88427-061-0.

Gartner (2019), PPM tools overview: https://www.gartner.com/reviews/market/project-portfolio-management-worldwide

Gartner (2019), PPM tools Magic Quadrant: https://www.gartner.com/en/documents/3917095/magic-quadrant-for-project-and-portfolio-management

Gartner (2020), client survey: https://www.gartner.com/en/newsroom/press-releases/2020-06-24-gartner-hr-survey-finds-52--of-organizations--busines

Goldratt, Eliyahu M. (1997). Critical chain. *Great Barrington, Massachusetts: North River Press.* ISBN 0-88427-153-6.

Harvard Business Review (2020) client survey: https://hbr.org/2020/06/3-things-youre-getting-wrong-about-organizational-change

Mintzberg, Henry (1978). "Patterns in Strategy Formation" (PDF). *Management Science. 24 (9): 934–48.* doi:10.1287/mnsc.24.9.934. *Archived from the original (PDF) on 19 October 2013.* Retrieved 31 August 2012.

Porter, Michael E. (1979). "How Competitive Forces Shape Strategy", *Harvard Business Review*, 1979 (Vol. 57, No. 2), pp. 137-145.

Porter, Michael E. (1985). Competitive Advantage: Creating and Sustaining Superior Performance. *New York: Simon and Schuster.* ISBN 9781416595847. Retrieved 9 September 2013.

The Association for Project Management (APM) conditions for project success; https://www.apm.org.uk/media/1621/conditions-for-project-success_web_final_0.pdf

The Standish Group CHAOS report
https://www.standishgroup.com/sample_research

World Economic Forum (January 2020)
https://www.weforum.org/agenda/2019/12/business-trends-for-next-10-years/

Printed in Great Britain
by Amazon